EDUCATING MARSTON

A Mother and Son's Journey through Autism

CHRISTINE WEISS
and Eric Weiss, MD

The information provided in this book is designed to provide helpful information on the subjects discussed. This book is not meant to be used, nor should it be used, to diagnose or treat any medical condition. For the diagnosis or treatment of any medical problem, consult your own physician or practitioner. The publisher and author are not responsible for any specific health or allergy needs that may require medical attention or supervision and are not liable for any damages or negative consequences from any treatment, action, application, or preparation given to any person reading or following the information in this book. References are provided for informational purposes only and do not constitute endorsement of any websites or other sources. Readers should be aware that the websites listed in this book may change.

Published by

Changing Lives Press
P.O. Box 140189 • Howard Beach, NY 11414
www.changinglivespress.org

ISBN: 978-099862314-6

Cover Design: Claire Moore
Interior Design: Lauren Michelle
Cover Photo: LizPiercePhotography.com

For Dawne: Thank you to my best friend for truth, guidance, and unwavering love. I love you.

For William: Thank you for becoming part of our family. You've always treated Marston like a brother. I love you.

For Austin: Thank you for your love, understanding, sacrifice, and compassion. You are a remarkable and beautiful man. I love you more.

For Eric: Thank you for your love and understanding, and the dedication to research and validating all the therapies I've found throughout the years. You are the rock of our family. I love you forever.

.°.°.°.

A special thanks to all the teachers, therapists, and caregivers who worked tirelessly to make Marston who he is today.

Especially thank you to Karin Hunt, for taking Marston into your classroom and home, treating him like your own, and for doing "whatever it takes." You are an amazing teacher, person, and mother.

A NOTE TO THE READERS

I believe I'm here to help others as I have been both helped and blessed spiritually along the way. It's taken me twenty years to gather the information in this book—a roadmap of a mother and son's journey with autism. I have been shown the way, and my gift back to the world is to serve as a guide for anyone I can.

—Christine Weiss

EDUCATING MARSTON

CHRISTINE WEISS

CONTENTS

INTRODUCTION

As a mom of a child with special needs, I'm drawn to stories like *Mask* and *What's Eating Gilbert Grape*. I recently saw the movie *Wonder*. I "get" these stories. But, unlike with my situation, with the boy in *Wonder*, there was protocol. That child had a physical deformity. My husband, Eric, is a plastic surgeon who works on cases like that. *"We're going to do A, B, C...."* Eric maps out a plan to right the wrong nature (or an accident) has done, like in the story *Wonder*. Even when there are no medical procedures available to help someone with a physical deformity, it's still apparent that this person is different, and—this is significant—it's generally apparent as to why.

My son, Marston, is beautiful. He's a handsome young man by anybody's standards. He looks normal. Then, you talk to Marston, and you realize that, while he's not exactly "abnormal," he's not exactly normal. He speaks differently than the average person and has unusual quirks, too. And, even though you can't put a label on what's amiss, you know something doesn't feel right. There's an imaginary wall, a clear piece of glass, separating Marston from normal.

It's hard being a parent to a child with autism—but not because I don't love my child. He is my heart. It's isolating and confusing and heartbreaking to look at your perfect child with everything in the right place, except that it's not.

I'm a spiritual person. I believe God has molded me into the person I am today through my child. I smile easily. I look on the bright side because that's who I am. When people meet me, learn our story, and see my light and positivity, they ask, "Would you change your son if you could?" (My disposition, once again, has been mistaken for complacency.) To them, I respond, "Absolutely! If your child had cancer, would you change it if you could?" There's not a rational parent on the planet that wouldn't seek treatment for a child with a disorder or disease if treatment or a cure were available.

But I was chosen for this battle—and make no mistake, it is a battle. It's my life's purpose. My efforts and faith have given me strength to accept the situation, not back down from it. That will never happen. I would give my blood and my breath for Marston to experience life as a normal kid.

Marston was born before Google and Facebook were invented. But, forget about technology for a second. Cancer, from the Greek word *karkinos*, was discovered around 1600 BC, over 3,500 years ago. The first case of autism was documented less than one hundred years ago. This is how little we know.

You can't google "cures for autism." Well, that's not true; you can google anything, and I've plugged "autism" into the search bar about a million times, give or take, since the explosion of the World Wide Web. Except it doesn't lead me to the answers I'm seeking. There are plenty of hits on different therapies, but no cure. The symbol for autism is a puzzle piece. Each autistic person's experience with the disorder is individual, unique as a snowflake.

"Do you have friends with normal kids?" That's another question I get a lot.

Before Marston was born, I didn't know anyone who had a child with autism. Looking back, I see that my life as a wife and new mom wasn't just normal but easy, at least by comparison. I was married to a wonderful man. We had a wonderful child, Austin, our first son. He was the healthy baby every parent dreams about. I didn't think too much about it then, about my easy life. But, to answer the question: Yes, I have close friends who have so-called normal kids, and they love and support Marston and me daily. However, my fellow warrior moms are in a different category; they understand and live the battle. It is these moms I call when I'm down. I would take these women to war with me.

When you have a child with a diagnosis of autism—or anywhere on the autism spectrum disorder—you learn fast who your real friends are. You learn some other things, too: Your child will be growing up without friends. He won't be invited to any parties or playdates. No one will be coming to his birthday parties. Many of your friends with the so-called normal kids will go away because it's just too hard to be around people that are different. It's too much work.

I imagine regular parents of regular kids have found the idea of hanging out with Marston uncomfortable, and so they've avoided it. Why should their beautiful, perfect child be put in an awkward situation, even if it's for just a couple hours at a little boy's birthday party? What did their healthy child do wrong to be punished in that way? Nothing. We all look at life through our own lenses. There's no blame here. This reality is no one's fault.

When I was in my twenties, I had the white-picket-fence kind of life many women dream about. Not anymore. Life is still beautiful, however messy, but nothing's perfect, and the majority of my friends are warriors. They're raising children who are unique and special. My friends fight every day for their children, and they fight for mine, too. They sleep with swords, and they rise at dawn with their armor on. They do this without complaint. I thank God for these friends every day.

When I leave this earth, I want to know I've done everything I can to create awareness for autism and to find a cure. I want moms who have kids on the autism spectrum to hand this book to their mothers, sisters, neighbors, friends, and I want them to say, "Read this and you'll understand." Eric said he'll practice medicine until he's eighty if he has to. It takes money, after all, to fight this battle…a lot of money!

For twenty-three years, there's been a piece of glass separating Marston from the rest of the world. My promise to my son and to every child like him is that I won't stop fighting until I've shattered it.

AUTISM STATS

Autism used to affect 1/10,000 babies through the seventies. By the nineties, that statistic was 1/1,000. It's diagnosed four times as often in males. (While rarer in girls, they seem to be affected more severely, exhibiting extreme symptoms.) As of this writing, 1/59 births in the US result in an ASD [Autism Spectrum Disorder] diagnosis.

EDUCATING MARSTON

PART I

A Mother and Son's Journey

1

LIFE IN FIFTH GEAR

> "What really matters in life, is what we do with
> what we know."
>
> —Oprah

I WAS BARRELING DOWN I-95 in the breakdown lane, hoping a cop would pull me over. Five weeks before my due date, I'd gone into labor. Eric was in surgery, a long and difficult case. He wasn't going to be available for hours. We hadn't even lived in Florida for a year, meaning I didn't know who to call when I couldn't reach my husband. So, there I was, driving myself to Baptist Hospital in downtown Jacksonville, scared, crying, praying—about as panicked as a person could be.

Let me back up for a minute....

Upon receiving his undergraduate degree in chemistry, Eric was awarded a United States Health Professional Scholarship, which paid for Duke University Medical School. After Duke, there were five years of general surgery residency at University of California, San Francisco. Two years of plastic surgery training at the University of Miami followed that. Then, the Navy owned him. We wanted to move somewhere that felt more permanent for raising a family, so Eric put in a request for Navy Hospital, Jacksonville, and it was accepted. The catch was we had to move right away. In the summer of '94, we found a cute, little house and, a month later, moved to Ponte Vedra Beach, a small town between Jacksonville and St. Augustine. We soon found out I was expecting our second child.

Austin was five. I enrolled him in a kindergarten class at Ponte Vedra Elementary. I remember meeting his first teacher, Miss Baxter. She noticed that Austin seemed extra bright for a kid his age. They'd later have him tested and inform us that he would benefit from being in a classroom setting designed for gifted students. I remember thinking how awesome it was that my child got his daddy's big brain.

I wanted to do all things new moms do to ensure their child would be loved, protected, and have the best upbringing possible, so I became a room mom. Watching Miss Baxter in action with young kids every day was nothing short of inspiring. Even though she was the first teacher I'd ever been around as a parent, I knew she was top notch.

And life went on without any speed bumps until March 17, 1995, St. Patrick's Day.

It was a Friday. I dropped Austin off at school but didn't go in to be the room mom, as I had a routine OB appointment scheduled.

It was supposed to be a regular checkup. When I got there, the doctor asked the typical "how are you feeling today?" question. I had noticed that it felt as if I couldn't control my bladder that morning, like I was leaking urine a little bit or something. With Austin, the pregnancy had been wonderfully uneventful. I gained the right amount of weight and experienced all the other things that happen to a woman when she's pregnant—the first-trimester fatigue, moodiness, a bit of morning sickness, heartburn in the last trimester. It all went down just as the books said it would. I carried him to term, too.

The doctor gave me an examination and said my membranes had ruptured prematurely. I needed to get to the hospital immediately, as I was about to have the baby. It was five weeks shy of my due date. To say I became panicked is an understatement. My doctor then took a sonogram and assured me that Marston was approximately six pounds and six ounces, and that his lungs were fully developed. There were no reassuring words beyond that—just a "get to the hospital as quickly as possible" directive.

As the wife of a surgeon, I often couldn't get in touch with Eric, and I rarely knew the exact time he'd be coming home. That was standard. I think it was probably everything that day, though, that had me so on edge. The "you're in labor" diagnosis, combined with living in a new place and Eric being unreachable—it was a lot for this young mom.

So, there I was, cruising in the breakdown lane on I-95. People must have thought I was nuts. I don't remember much about the drive there; adrenaline does that. I remember repeating "God, I hope they know I'm coming" over and over again for some reason.

Nurses and medics were waiting for me with a wheelchair at the ready.

"Hop in, Mrs. Weiss. We're taking you upstairs to the maternity ward."

I puked on the way up, several times.

The nurse checked my cervix and started Pitocin.

Still no Eric.

That's when I remembered Austin was still at school—oh, my goodness. This was before cellphones were common. But, thankfully, I had all the important phone numbers in my life memorized. I was supposed to be at school, lined up with the other moms in the circular drive pickup point, with a number and photo of Austin on the dash that corresponded to the "Austin" waiting on the curb. Even though there were about fourteen kids to a class and everyone knew everyone, Ponte Vedra Elementary had all their procedures down to a science. Despite the madness, I retrieved the number from memory and called. Miss Baxter told me not worry, that she would take Austin to her house. She would end up keeping him for the next three days. She became the first warrior in our lives.

She was an angel, our angel, and we're friends to this day. Years later, she married a wonderful man, Gene Weiss (no relation), becoming a Mrs. Weiss herself.

And then, Eric arrived. He basically slid into home as I crowned and gave birth.

Marston's APGAR score was great. For anyone that doesn't know (or can't remember), the APGAR test happens one minute after birth, and then again five minutes after that. It stands for appearance, pulse, grimace, activity, and respiration. Marston weighed in at over six pounds and was 19.5 inches long, with a proportional and normal head circumference.

He had aspirated a small amount of amniotic fluid on the way out, which is sterile and not as worrisome as when babies aspirate meconium. The neonatologists reported Marston had mild sterile pneumonitis and put him on oxygen via nasal cannula, as he was having minor difficulty breathing.

He was slightly jaundiced, which was typical and manageable. At no point was Marston on a ventilator, but they kept him for four weeks. Aspirating amniotic fluid can affect the alveoli (microscopic air sacs where oxygen enters the blood) of the lungs, burning the delicate lining and making oxygen transfer more difficult, which is why he received oxygen via nasal cannula until May 25, one month after we took him home. Now, knowing all its benefits and connection to blood flow to the brain, we should have kept him on oxygen for a year. Who really knows; for every therapy, there are potential risks. But, like I mentioned, this was before cellphones and the explosion of the internet—before knowledge was an enter key away.

For the next month, I'd visit my baby during visiting hours. I wasn't allowed to breastfeed him, like I'd planned, like I had with Austin. I don't why. The nursing staff mentioned something about Marston expending too much energy. I guess he did not have enough stamina to suckle and breathe. To this day, I have anxiety about depriving him of the nutrients and healing potential of breast milk. The nurses did not encourage pumping, and, as a young mother, I did not question their authority.

Binding my breasts with compression wrap was awful. I was glad my sister, Margaret, was a delivery room nurse. She helped me considerably. Binding them didn't stop the leaking. And the process was painful to both my body and soul. I was a crazy hormonal mess, a wreck. I just wasn't getting to bond with my baby. I couldn't get close enough to Marston; it was the worst feeling in the world. And, I was never allowed to stay for as long as I would have preferred. It felt like a punishment. Visiting hours were limiting enough, but every time there was a blood draw, every time they fed Marston, every time the pediatric team was at his bedside, and during every nursing shift change, I was asked to leave. The nurturing was shattered.

Eric, being a doctor, wanted to know everything, as he understood doctor speak. He'd walk into the neonatal ICU (NICU), say hello, and pick up the chart. He'd go there at all hours of the day and night, as he wasn't generally available during business hours. He often came with specific questions concerning protocol. It was his son. His input and involvement were not well received. We all had the same goal. I never understood why the situation was always so tense. At one point, they stopped allowing him to look over Marston's medical chart.

One day, I went to the maternity ward, washed my hands, put on a sterile gown, smiled at the nurses on duty and the other mom preparing to visit her baby, and went into the NICU. Marston was gone from his crib, and his name had been erased from the baby board. I lost my breath and started to faint—went to my knees and actually blacked out. As I came to and fought back tears, a nurse came over. She told me he'd been moved to the NICU step-down unit. *Could someone have called? I truly thought he had died!*

Even through the tears, the fluctuations in my hormones, the constant feeling of life being out of control, the driving back and forth to and from the hospital (three, four times a day) just to see my newborn, I'd tell myself, "It's not about you. It's about Marston." I made this my mantra. "It's not about you."

I made tapes of the family talking or singing or reading a book to Marston. My voice, Eric's, Austin's, his grandmother's, his aunties'—we were all represented. Because he wasn't confined to an incubator, I could put the tape recorder in his crib. It was spacious enough, and I wanted him to have the comfort of his family's voices in that foreign environment. I even made a tape of my heartbeat. Newborns crave their mothers' touch, heartbeat, scent, and voice. It's all part of the bonding process. I asked the nurses to please, please play it when I wasn't around. I don't know if they ever did, but it was never on when I arrived.

When I think about this time in our lives, I still get a stomach ache. I'm right back there....

On my birthday, April 9, 1995, Marston received a hepatitis B vaccination while in the hospital. In Marston's case, since he was premature, this vaccine was given prior to his April 20 due date. He was still so immature. There was no signing of waivers, like nowadays. Even so, many moms are delirious enough after giving birth that they're not fully aware of what they're signing, anyway.

Eric and I believe this vaccination played a major role in Marston becoming autistic. In my gut, I know it's the reason. He was born under stressful circumstances but in good shape. He passed all the tests. He was never in an incubator, never intubated, never on a respirator. He only suffered from a mild, common issue and received the minimum amount of oxygen for it. He was thriving prior to this vaccination. It was plain to see he took a hit. Right after the vaccination, his oxygen requirements increased, his respiratory rate increased, he was given antibiotics, and we were all concerned he was becoming septic. His septic work-up turned up negative, meaning it was something else besides infection that was causing his body to suddenly react, to go into defense mode. He had a virus injected into his immature and already-stressed system and had a bad reaction to it; he was my baby and I could feel it. I watched the light leave his eyes. There was a Marston before the vaccination and a Marston after, one that was less alert.

I'm 100 percent for vaccinations—that is "safe vaccines." Eric and I both are. But I feel these vaccines need to be monovalent, in a single dose vial, and without preservatives. A monovalent vaccine immunizes against one particular strain of microorganism (or disease). This isn't even always an option. Medical research journalist Neil Z. Miller writes this in his 2016 article "Combining Childhood Vaccines at One Visit Is Not Safe" in the *Journal of American Physicians and Surgeons*:

> This CDC report also noted that "exposures to mixed stressors can produce health consequences that are additive, synergistic, antagonistic, or can potentiate the response expected from individual component exposures."[12] Thus, CDC is well aware that mixing several pharmaceutical products increases the likelihood of synergistic toxicity and unexpected adverse reactions. Nonetheless, CDC urges infants to receive multiple vaccines concurrently without scientific evidence to confirm the safety of this practice. Administering six, seven, or eight vaccine doses to an infant during a single physician visit is certainly more convenient

for parents, as opposed to making additional trips to the doctor's office, and increases the likelihood that the infant will receive all the vaccines, but vaccine safety must remain the highest priority.

Single dose vials are less likely to cause side effects or "synergistic toxicity" than multi-dose vials. Multi-dose vaccines require preservatives; monovalent vaccines do not require preservatives (such as the long-popular thimerosal, which contains mercury). Additionally, "Single-dose vaccine formats can prevent clinic-level vaccine wastage but may incur higher production, medical waste disposal, and storage costs than multi-dose formats." If vaccines were to be administered in single doses, the schedule would need to be customized and individualized for each child. This is what I'd like to see happen, because not every child is the same at three months, six months, nine months, etc. Treat the whole child. Hepatitis B is a sexually transmitted virus (or is transmitted by way of shared needles). There's no logical reason for an infant to be vaccinated against this, especially one so young. Marston had not even reached his calculated birth date. They wouldn't let me breastfeed him for fear it would cause too much stress on his system. Could we have waited until he was ten, or when he reached sexual maturity? His brain and immune system would have been developed. This only seems logical in the specific case of hep B. In Miller's article, he notes, when downloading and studying VAERS

(Vaccine Adverse Event Reporting System) reports from 1990–2010, there's a trend (an increase) in the number of vaccinations administered to an infant and their likelihood of having an adverse reaction with one exception: hep B. One dose of the hep B antigen created a disproportionately high percentage of infants in need of hospitalization due to adverse reaction compared to one dose of the other vaccinations in the report, making hep B an outlier in their study. (For the full article, the link is in Resources under Chapter 1 in the back of the book.) **For full article links and other general information, refer to the references and resources section in the back of the book.**

In the 1970s, the recommended vaccination list included vaccines for seven viruses/diseases that were combined for a total of three vaccinations:

- Polio vaccination
- Combined vaccination for tetanus, diphtheria, and pertussis (DTP vaccine)
- Combined vaccination for measles, mumps, and rubella (MMR vaccine).

The first hepatitis B vaccine became legal/licensed by the FDA in America in November 1981. By 1989, there were two hep B vaccines approved in the US. But, in 1990, CDC officials expressed concern that targeting high-risk individuals was an ineffective strategy to increase vaccination use and lower the incidence of hep B. So, by 1991, a universal hepatitis B vaccination was recommended for all US infants.

By the time Marston was born, in 1995, it was required in Florida. In 2002, it became mandatory that all mothers be tested for the virus as part of the prenatal exams. I was not tested for hepatitis B during either pregnancy (1989, 1995). Had I been, there would have been no reason to vaccinate my children, as I was neither a carrier nor at risk to become one. And, my baby was not sharing a needle or having sex, which sounds ridiculous even as I write it. But those are the only risk factors for developing hepatitis B.

There are thousands of arguments and articles written that fall on both sides of the hepatitis B-autism association with male neonates. But, in a cross-sectional study using weighted probability obtained from National Health Interview Survey 1997–2002 data sets, it was...

...concluded that parental report of autism diagnosis was determined to be three times higher than in full-term babies that weren't vaccinated for at least thirty days after birth. Vaccination status was determined from the vaccination record. Logistic regression was used to estimate the odds for autism diagnosis associated with neonatal hepatitis B vaccination among boys age 3–17 years, born before 1999, adjusted for race, maternal education, and two-parent household.

If we look at the history of vaccines in America, we can see how the vaccination schedule for our children has evolved.

In the early 1950s, four vaccines were available: diphtheria, tetanus, pertussis, and smallpox. Because three of these vaccines were combined into a single shot (DTP), children received five shots by the time they were two years old and not more than one shot at a single visit.

Nowadays, it's over triple that with multiple shots often administered per visit. Remember when the neighbor boy got the chickenpox and your mom said, "Get over there and hug Joey so we can get this over with." It's decades later; we're supposed to be more educated. What are we doing to our children's immune systems? We are weakening them.

Even now, with vaccinations in excess—a multi-billion-dollar industry—doctors still ask if you're feeling well prior to administering one, like the annual flu shot—which, by the way, isn't a vaccine against the winter flu virus. That virus hasn't yet hit; therefore, no one knows what its molecular composition will look like to create a vaccine to stop it. It's a gamble.

Sick babies and adults alike shouldn't have their bodies further burdened, as their systems are working overtime to heal something already. Marston's lungs were on the mend from sterile pneumonitis. He was a premature baby, a neonate. He was on oxygen. His system had enough to focus on.

You should have seen the palms of his hands and the bottoms of his feet—they were black and blue, covered in pinpricks from checking his oxygen, glucose, and hemoglobin daily. There was no speck of skin that hadn't been pricked by a needle since the day he was born. Marston had all he could manage before the vaccination. They had to resort to placing a heparin lock catheter in his scalp for blood draws, as his hands and feet were too beaten up from all the needles. They attempted to cover this intrusion with a small, knitted, baby blue hat.

For anyone interested in learning more about administering vaccinations the right way, Dr. Stephanie Cave wrote a book entitled *What Your Doctor May Not Tell You About Children's Vaccinations*. The book is informative and certainly not anti-vaccine, but Dr. Cave explains the pros and cons and gives parents the information to make responsible choices about vaccinating their children against the right kinds of viruses and diseases and foregoing the unnecessary vaccinations that just don't apply (like hep B, in our case). I attended a lecture she gave once, and this is a compelling and insightful read for parents and soon-to-be parents. I stand by her philosophy.

The bullet and the gun—apart, they are not dangerous, but together, they are a deadly combination. Infants that have come into the world under traumatic circumstances need time to allow for healing, time for their bodily systems to catch up, time for their immune systems to strengthen. "Being stressed and pairing that condition with a vaccine can result in disaster." This is the mantra of one of my fellow warrior moms, Leslie Weed.

Marston entered the world in fifth gear and, by the time we took him home, it was clear his life wasn't going to slow down anytime soon.

2

NO ONE LEFT BEHIND

"We can hurt and still do good for others."

—Joel Osteen
Your Best Life Now

I COME FROM A BIG, Catholic family of five sisters and one brother: Margaret, Peter, Sallie, Patty, me, and Paula. We lived in Bradford, Massachusetts. My dad, Stanley Marston, was a successful business owner. My mother, Barbara, was happy being a mom. Actually, at the time, my mother was always happy. We were a lucky family living in an upper-middle-class neighborhood. My early childhood was damned-near flawless. Being the youngest—"the baby"—for the first six years of my life, boy, I was spoiled. And, as you can imagine, Peter, being the only boy, was the apple of everyone's eye.

My mother would never admit this in a million years, but I'm almost certain my little sister, Paula, who's six years my junior, was what people in those days referred to as a "surprise." Still, she was one more person to love in the Marston family and a delight for all.

Winters can be tough in the New England states, as anyone who's lived there knows. In February of 1964, we had one of the worst storms of the century. On this night, with my parents at a neighbor's home, Peter and Sallie were in the house babysitting their three younger siblings—Patty, me, and Paula.

Paula was eighteen months old and had come down with a typical winter cold, so Peter and Sallie were especially watchful. Sallie went to check on her and came back yelling, "She's purple!" Paula was dazed, eyes open, but unresponsive to touch or sound, not even responding to her name. Peter ran next door and alerted my parents. There was no calling 911; it wasn't established until 1968. No one was going out in that storm. It took forever for my parents to drive her to the hospital.

Paula survived the seizure but was never the same. As the months passed, the toddler that used to know her colors, numbers, and letters barely spoke. Her light had gone out. Her brain had been deprived of oxygen; there was no going back to the bright and rambunctious Paula my mother had given birth to.

Being the closest in age, I started watching over my sister, helping Mom daily. One second, I was the baby, getting all the attention—then, Paula the happy surprise arrived, and, within three years, she had become a special needs child. The attention that had enriched my young life vanished. It was an adjustment. But, back in the day, in a Catholic family especially, you did what you were told, what had to be done, and so, I fell in line without skipping a beat. (No one was sitting around talking about their feelings or complaining about what was or wasn't fair in my house.)

Before Paula's illness, my mom was what you'd call a country club wife. It was the sixties. Women whose husbands were financially successful men such as doctors, lawyers, and business owners were women with status. They had reputations to uphold. Whether you were comfortable in knit suits, hose and pumps, and making bi-weekly trips to the hair salon hardly mattered. It's what the socialite wives did back then. They played the part, baked the tuna casseroles, gathered at the local country club, drank the designated Canadian Club and water in a highball glass (as they had their waistlines to watch); they walked the walk. My mother's circle of friends all looked smartly put together and perfectly coiffed. I remembered thinking how fun it was going to be to grow up, dress so pretty, and have the perfect family. We even summered at a cottage in West Yarmouth, a village on the Cape, not far from the Kennedy compound. We'd see them out on their boat. We weren't super rich; we were from Massachusetts, and that's what people did in the summer. Everybody, it seemed, followed the social norms of the time to a T.

Then the storm struck, and everything changed, including my mother's status among her group of gals. It was hard for her to be showy with a mentally handicapped child clinging to her leg. Mom got pressured about putting Paula into an institution. *Why on earth would anyone go out in public with a child like that?* It was shameful.

The Kennedys defined America, and especially Massachusetts by that point—meaning, the pressure wasn't coming from just her inner circle.

.°.°.°.

In 1918, Rose (Fitzgerald) Kennedy gave birth to her second daughter, Rose Marie "Rosemary" Kennedy. During the birthing process, Rose had been instructed not to push for nearly two hours. The baby's head was stuck inside the birth canal and lost vital oxygen to the brain.

Rosemary wasn't like the other kids. She was a true beauty, but, at maturity, she had the IQ and mentality of an average ten-year-old, making it difficult to fold her into the Kennedys' dense, ongoing social schedule. When she was younger, she tagged along fine, with a brother or sister working to blend her quietly into the shadows of their high-profile lifestyle. But, when puberty hit, it came with violent, emotional outbursts, making it impossible to pass her off as so-called normal.

The cure for Rosemary, doctors suggested in the early 1940s, was a procedure they called a lobotomy. Rosemary's father, Joseph P. Kennedy, set up the operation without his wife's knowledge. James W. Watts and Walter Freeman performed the surgery while Rosemary was under mild sedation. A twenty-three-year-old Rosemary was instructed to say the Lord's Prayer over and over while the doctors made a small incision in the top frontal part of her brain and swung a knife back and forth across her gray matter until the prayer became unintelligible garble. She had the mentality of a two-year-old after that and became incontinent. After being confined to a convent during her teen years, Rosemary would spend the rest of her life, until her death at the age of eighty-six, in isolation in a mental institution.

The Kennedys modeled how to treat children with disabilities, and America followed suit.

Shortly after Rosemary's lobotomy, in 1943, Psychiatrist Leo Kannar from Johns Hopkins University identified autism as a distinct neurological condition. He added, however, that he noticed these children seemed to be the product of educated but unaffectionate parents. The mothers were particularly cold. He suggested this intellectual (uncaring) approach to parenting likely played a role in the disorder, and he coined the term "refrigerator mothers." So catchy was this phrase, it evolved into a psychiatric norm over the next couple decades.

The phrase came back around in the nineties as a way to deflect from vaccinations playing a role in the increase in autism.

Terms like refrigerator moms are attention grabbing. It's a distraction, a way to place blame safely—and, by "safely," I mean without affecting the economy. If something like vaccinations were the cause or partially the cause, holding X percentage of the blame for the rise in autism, can you imagine what that would do to pharmaceutical companies?

This isn't a book that's intended to be controversial; this is me telling you all I know—my heart and my mind are here on every page of Marston's story—so that you can find your power. This information and these statistics are all part of the empowerment process.

Shame and blame were how kids with special needs were handled for the better part of the twentieth century. We've made strides in many ways since Rosemary and my sister, but we have a long way to go.

•º•º•º•

Even though my mother had never complained about caring for Paula, she put her into an institution at the urgings of her peers and her doctor at Boston Children's Hospital. Paula was just five years old.

She was taken to Danvers State Hospital. This hospital, really an asylum, a scary brick monstrosity, was built in 1874. My mother, a friggin' saint who personified joy prior to that, cried the entire time Paula was gone. She was completely inconsolable.

After a week without Paula, she piled us in the station wagon. Remember those? I was in the very back, facing the cars behind us—dead for sure if we were to get hit, but happy for the view and the adventure of a long car trip (oblivious to the destination).

An hour into our journey, Mom turned up a long drive that led us through a forest of silver birch trees in bloom. As the warm breeze blew, the leaves on the trees shimmered, reflecting the sun. *Trees dripping with diamonds*, I innocently mused. It was magical. Mom parked, and we all got out in front of the ominous, red brick building. It was isolated in rural Massachusetts. The whimsical feeling the silver birch trees had inspired vanished in a snap. The fairy tale part of our adventure was over. We lined up and followed Mom up the brick stairs.

We went through one locked door, then another, then another. Patients in straightjackets lined the walls: standing, lying, screaming, crying, sleeping, drugged to no end.

We found Paula's room. She was strapped to a bed and all drugged up, too. Mom released her, pulled her into her arms, and carried her out. We all followed in amazement. I remember it to this day—the horror as well as the heroism.

"Nemo Resideo." No One Left Behind. Like the Marines, that had always been my mother's mindset. She was a saint and a warrior, and she proved it that day.

Later, she'd tell us we were brought to the institution to understand what Paula's life would have been like had we not rescued her. She told us to think about that place when we grew tired of listening to the repetition and the fits or when we were sick of the chaotic madness that Paula brought to our household. Paula had a habit of taking our music boxes and tossing the jewelry in them out the bedroom window. During wintertime, this was especially annoying. We'd find our special trinkets and jewelry after the spring thaw. It was one of many types of episodes we learned to endure.

"Think about that hell on earth and thank God we are better, stronger, and built with more compassion. The Marstons take care of each other," Mom reminded us.

And we did; we thought about it, we understood, and we took care of each other.

With degrees from outstanding universities and colleges, including PhDs and masters, we were a bright family with means; we were also a family that cared for a beautiful child with special needs. And we became a family that suffered great loss when Peter, my only brother, died tragically in a motorcycle accident at the age of twenty-one. It was hell, and that further changed the Marston family dynamic. But, we would continue to be people who loved hard, complained little, and pitched in equally. My mother worked long and hard hours, over decades, educating Paula.

My sister now lives in a group home and goes to a job every day. She has friends, purpose, and she's happy. She has a good attitude. With my parents gone, it's up to us siblings to take care of her and love her, and we do.

The life of my oldest son has run parallel in so many ways with that of my own childhood. Austin, too, was born into the circumstance of having a sibling with special needs. He was also six years old when it happened. My time as his mother was cut short, stolen from him while he was only in elementary school. One second, I was a room mom; I was the mom other moms would work to emulate, which was, after all, my big plan back then—to be this perfect role model of a mother. I was going to give my oldest son the world. The next second, all my time and energy was devoted to educating Marston.

That second has stretched into decades. Austin's had to assume a caregiving role from the start. It wasn't voluntary.

When Eric and I pass from this place, he will be in charge of caring for Marston. It will be his burden—caregiver for life—and he doesn't have three other siblings who will be there to help.

There are no words to express my deep gratitude for his sacrifices. I'm thankful to understand my oldest son's position in our family from a sibling's perspective, but I could write a hundred books and dedicate every one of them to Austin, and it wouldn't be enough. Austin's DNA, like mine, imparts the love and bond of family; he's always been so compassionate, a natural-born caregiver. In other words, he was bred and molded for this gig. For that, I'm grateful.

God would send another special angel to help with Marston: William.

Austin met William at YMCA summer camp the first year we were in Ponte Vedra. We would end up becoming next-door neighbors. William became Austin's best friend and, eventually, one of the family. He grew up with Marston, too. William would help with therapy and take on the roles of teacher, mentor, and second older brother.

I consider William my son to this day, blood or not. He is our family.

3

THE WONDER YEARS

"To all mothers in every circumstance, including those who struggle—and all will—I say, be peaceful. 'Be peaceful. Believe in God and yourself. You are doing better than you think you are.'"

—Jeffrey R. Holland
"Behold Thy Mother"

ERIC'S MOTHER WAS JEWISH AND his father Catholic. Knowing that pleasing both sides of the family would be near impossible, they decided to raise their kids Lutheran. His mom was a psychologist, and this was her way of exposing her family to various religions, educating them to the fullest. To say Eric is a spiritually open-minded person is an understatement. Because I was raised Catholic, and because his family was so relaxed and enlightened about the practice of religion, we decided to raise our kids Catholic upon his mother's recommendation. She believed that marriage could withstand the rigors of life more successfully if husband and wife were of the same faith. Eric spent several months studying Catholicism to convert.

As soon as Marston was home from his five-week stay at the hospital, getting him baptized was at the top of the list. We set a date. As the day grew close, we met with our priest. He said there was a new guy in town who was being ordained a deacon and asked if it would be okay if he performed Marston's baptism as his first formal sacrament. That sounded lovely to us. We said yes.

We met Father Cowart the morning before the ceremony. He wasn't a younger priest but a man of fifty, switching careers to follow a calling. Eric and I really liked this guy; he was so charismatic, and we were excited to have him be a part of Marston's journey, as well as Marston being pivotal in his.

After the ceremony, we asked if we could take a picture of just him and Marston. Then, we said our goodbyes, and everybody wished everybody well.

…So, I have this thing about *thank you* cards. I love writing a good, old-fashioned note of thanks. (This was commonplace back in 1995, but I still try to do it to this day.) So, as soon as I got the photos from Marston's baptism developed, I made a duplicate of the picture of Father Cowart holding Marston and added it to his *thank you* note. Father Cowart had left town by that point, so I got his address from the parish office and popped it in the mail.

This was the first and last celebrated event in Marston's life where people thought—*assumed*—he was normal.

.°.°.°.

(Please forgive me in advance on some of these timelines—from 1995 through 1999, life was a blur.)

At around six months old, we started Marston in **Gymboree** classes three days a week because I didn't see him responding to me or moving in ways that seemed natural based on raising Austin and being around other babies. The classes were somewhat successful because they were social outings and provided stimulation to a growing brain. However, I could see he was behind his peers, even then.

By Christmastime (at nine months old), he was thinking about crawling and started shortly thereafter, around ten months. That was a relief. He was eating well. As a dietician, I had already instituted a gluten-free and casein-free diet. He was not eating baby food from a jar or anything processed; I pureed his food much like a mama bird. He could transfer his playthings from hand to hand, an indicator of physical well-being at that age. That was a relief, too. And, he wasn't unhappy. I'd call him perfectly content, even though he was in his own world. Still, he never reached for me, and there was almost no language and no eye contact. It seemed when he had ten words, his peers had 200 words. There was no catching up, just falling further behind.

When Marston turned one, on March 17, 1996, I contacted a **neurologist**. He was examined by Dr. Harry Abrams on July 15, 1996. On August 8, his brain activity (EEG) came back normal. His physical skills were all pretty much on task. Dr. Abrams said Marston had "neuro-typical development" for a child his age, and he added that he seemed "happy." But, we decided to have **genetic testing** done, as well as a **hearing test**.

After a plethora of tests, there were no genetic or hearing abnormalities.

By eighteen months, when I knew for certain we were in trouble, I started **speech therapy** with **Nancy Lotowitz**. Knowing a dozen words or more; putting two or more words together, such as "all done!"; having an innate understanding of intonation and using it effectively; using body language to convey what a limited vocabulary cannot—these are some of the things that equate to normal cognitive development of an average eighteen-month-old. Marston wasn't doing any of it.

He had started walking at seventeen months. This was hopeful, as walking, like "reaching for mom," was on my new list of milestones (or miracles) for my second son. But, there was minimal speech. He spoke occasionally in what I'd call garble that was directed at no one and nothing. Aside from that, I was blind to what he needed beyond food, clothing, and shelter to survive. Speech therapy was beneficial, but I knew he needed more intensive therapies. This was the tip of the iceberg.

In January of 1997, when Marston was about twenty months old, I enrolled him in **Kindermusik.**

This method of early childhood education—founded in Germany but coming to the USA in 1970—is devoted to teaching children from infancy through age seven how to focus, learn, and respond through music. The program's intent is to introduce babies and children to the sounds of music. Movement, singing, games, and even playing instruments—along with parent or caregiver involvement—are the tools instructors use throughout any given class period. The program is broken down further by age, capitalizing on different things as a baby grows into a toddler and so on. The focus of the class was enhancing communication skills, self-confidence, and self-control from eighteen months to the age of three. The Kindermusik International philosophy is that music therapy can spark the brain to be more open to learning and communicating effectively, but they know there is no greater outside force to assist in brain growth and development than the home environment. For this reason, the primary guardian/caregiver is advised to participate and learn the method intimately.

Marston loved this class. He could jump and move around and he's always loved music.

Concurrently, we started **Mommy & Me** classes three days a week. I don't remember them as well. I do recall them reinforcing how far behind he was compared to other children his age, but I don't remember what was done to accommodate our situation. I just knew those classes weren't good for my psyche or Marston's, and it didn't take us long to move on. Mommy & Me did solidify the notion that the answers I was seeking weren't going to come easy, and it felt like time was against us. The longer we stayed in the dark, the longer Marston remained isolated. And, by that point, one thought punctuated all others: *This is bad, this is really bad.*

Just before Marston was two, I enrolled him in **Accotink Academy** three mornings a week. This was a neighborhood school, just two minutes from the house in Ponte Vedra. It had a very low student-to-teacher ratio.

Accotink Academy believes each child has his or her own developmental calendar and that the educational and emotional potential for every child is different. Reaching each child's potential at every stage of the learning game is the goal of this academy. Their program capitalizes on understanding the different learning abilities within everyone. It places importance on increasing the confidence of each student with the goal that every human can be a productive part of society, regardless of any natural-born deficits in "normal" development.

This school had certified teachers, a therapeutic support staff, OTs, and clinical psychologists on site. They were dedicated to kids with learning disabilities and kids on the autism spectrum disorder.

I believe in schools like this, but, for us at the time, there was little to no visible improvement in Marston's focus or capabilities. He went in not being able to communicate, and there were no improvements in that regard. He still had little to no language skills and made no eye contact. The atmosphere appeared to create more chaos for him, as there was too much distraction. His sensory issues, communication skills, and general mannerisms were even more skewed (or heightened) after a day at school. He appeared to be displaying symptoms of ADD, as well. This was obvious when he was alone at home with me or one of our helpers. This particular academy was new to the area and still finding its bearings. That may have had an effect on kids like Marston—kids on the spectrum that needed one-on-one time constantly to achieve even minute advancements with cognition and motor skills—but the environment didn't work for Marston specifically.

We left the school after five months in order to start full-time speech, physical, and occupational therapies. I had finally realized how far behind he was, and that it was up to me to "catch him up."

To recap, by the first two years of Marston's life, he'd undergone these tests and been enrolled in these classes:

- Neurological testing
- Genetic testing
- Hearing testing

- Gymboree
- Mommy & Me
- Speech therapy
- Kindermusik
- Accotink Academy

Unfortunately, the reality is that therapy costs money. Eric was in the Navy and had to take a second job working in local emergency rooms so we could continue to pursue these treatments. We had paid $100,000 in medical care and schooling since Marston's birth (in twenty-two months). It's important that money is discussed, too, to understand the full scope of stressors that parents of kids with disabilities deal with daily.

Needless to say, I was looking forward to his two-year checkup. I felt confident that I'd been doing my part to help my son in every conceivable way. Marston had undergone or been enrolled in every test, therapy, or program I could find using "the world" now as my library, thanks to the internet. In addition, I was doing at-home therapy after digesting the information or techniques to complement these treatments. And, I was reading any and all child-development literature that had been published since the dawn of time. Nothing had an impact, so, I was excited to get some real answers from a pediatric professional, as I'd hit a dead end with the neurologist and everything else.

In the spring of 1997, the doctor looked him over, weighed, and measured him. He tossed Marston a ball. Marston caught it. And, when prompted to throw it back, he did. Then, he told me Marston was a late bloomer.

After that single, cognitive observation and generalized comment, he then wrote "MR" on my son's chart. Mentally retarded. It killed me. I tried as best I could to make him understand that something had happened to Marston. He wasn't the baby I'd given birth to. Even though I'd only had a few weeks with that baby, it lingered in my mind. Whenever I expressed that, however, I sounded crazy and generally got ignored; this time was no exception. Marston was finally walking, thank goodness, but there was still no speech. He was content, mostly, but I saw his frustration. Even Marston knew there was a disconnect between what was going on in his young brain and what he could relay to me or anyone. Children that are "late bloomers" are expressive: happy, sad, mad....

Marston didn't understand how to be expressive, and I could see and feel that; yet, I was helpless. The pain of watching my son from the other side of the glass is something I will never be able to describe, as I have yet to find a word to accurately articulate that emotion. In a small way, this made me feel connected to him, especially in these early years. He couldn't reach me, and I couldn't reach anyone about what was going on with him. We were united in our frustration. At least there was that.

My life was devoted to Marston, but when I wasn't working directly with him or on his behalf, I was observing the world of babies and toddlers around me. And, when I wasn't doing either of those things, I was reading on the topics of autism and other possible syndromes, defects, or diseases, and on the myriad of therapies and treatments.

Our pediatrician was basically an ass in both his treatment of me and assessment of Marston that day. He chalked Marston's delays up to a low IQ and sent us on our way. He gave me no direction when I asked him about therapies and other interventions. He brushed me off. It was so infuriating. I wasted two hours of our precious time on that appointment. I could have been walking with Marston. We could have been listening to classical music or playing with his colored blocks. I could have been smiling and saying "I love you" over and over, hoping for a smile in return.

While autism diagnoses were unfortunately growing in popularity, there was no such thing as a spectrum disorder. Understanding of the disorder was still in the infancy stage.

As any parent knows, life goes into panic mode when a child is sick. For two years, my adrenaline was running on high; it had me wiped out all the time. I never really slept, and, when I was awake, my job was singular in focus: get through to Marston.

Meanwhile, Eric was focused on providing for the family, working double time. That left Austin with a dad that kissed him goodnight after he was in bed most nights and a mom that I referred to as Tired Mom. But, Tired Mom was thankful for how easy my first-born son was. That was never an issue. To this day, I look back amazed at his maturity and thoughtfulness at such a young age. I had become obsessed with breaking the glass wall, and, instinctually, Austin must have picked up on that and supported my efforts by steering clear of my mission.

As I sat at home that evening after Marston's checkup, cup of tea in hand, staring at the living room wall and waiting for Eric to come home from surgery, I realized it was official: no one knew what was wrong with Marston.

I was on my own.

I don't want any parent to ever feel as small and alone as I did that night. Alone in their fight.

•º•º•º•

These are some symptoms that indicate a child may have autism spectrum disorder (ASD):

- Does not speak as well as other kids their age or does not speak at all
- Poor eye contact or no eye contact
- Does not respond to their name
- May walk on toes or may not walk at all
- Lost in his or her own world

- Tunes others out/appears withdrawn
- Does not understand when to smile socially or may not understand how to smile
- Unable to express wants and needs
- Cannot follow simple commands
- May exhibit unusually long and severe temper tantrums
- May exhibit repetitive or odd behaviors
- May show an unusual attachment to inanimate objects, especially hard ones (e.g., prefers a plastic cup over a blanket)
- Prefers to play alone

4

YOU CAN DO IT

"Every day, we can be someone's miracle."

—Anonymous

GIVING BIRTH TO AND NURTURING a child is second nature for many women. I remember breastfeeding Austin, his soft, warm, precious, little hands pressing into my skin, his wide, innocent eyes looking up at me—I was his whole world. I'd watch his tears dry and hear his cries soften into coos as I scooped him into my arms, rescuing him from a bad dream. I would bring him into our bed, place him between us to feel the security and love, and he would react as babies do when they feel the parent-child bond instinctually.

Austin spent a lot of time observing me, curious boy that he was. I delighted in that. The everyday stuff, it was so easy. I didn't even think about it. I certainly didn't consider any of it miraculous beyond life itself being a miracle. I thought it was natural. Like breathing. I had taken the mom-baby bond for granted.

With Marston, well, nothing was natural. I'd start every morning by telling myself that today was the day I was going to look into Marston's eyes and he was going to look back and want me, really want me—his mom. Today, he would reach for me. I would see him smile for the first time. Walk. He'd say, "Mama," "Daddy," or even "ball"—*that's going to happen today.* I believed this because I had prayed about it the night before. "Dear, God, when I wake up tomorrow and put my child in my arms, give me a sign, any sign that he understands, that he knows he's loved. He can trust me, after all, I'm Mom. I'll take any silly sign, anything at all. Thank you in advance."

In a matter of months, Marston would be three, and I would have uttered that same, sad prayer a thousand times. That prayer was getting really old.

Inhale, hold, exhale, repeat. Can you imagine if you had to remind yourself to breathe—inhale, hold, exhale, repeat? If every time you took a breath of life, you had to do it consciously? It would get exhausting fast. That's what it was like trying to be a mom to a baby that appeared to want something, like babies do, but it wasn't me. I hadn't a clue what Marston needed. There was nothing natural about it. It was terrifying. I knew I couldn't keep doing this day in, day out. My threshold was near. I didn't know what was on the other side of it, though—this breaking point. Maybe insanity? I'm sure I looked like hell, too, even though people were kind in that regard.

I had a support system, at least; for that, I was grateful. Looking back at this fragile time, I've wondered how single moms and parents without extended family (especially family nearby) ever get through those initial years.

My parents were living in Clearwater. It was a four-hour drive, so we saw them more sporadically. But Mom called to check on Marston regularly. On March 20, 1998, just a few days after Marston's birthday, Mom called per usual. But, instead of jumping into typical conversation, she proceeded to tell me that Dad had become acutely sick and was in the intensive care unit. Eric and I packed up the car and left.

Thank goodness Eric was with me. He was able to assist the nurses with my dad's pain management, as it was obvious he didn't have long to live. He was in the ICU on a ventilator. I crawled into bed with him, knowing this was it. "You're so lucky, Dad," I whispered. "You're going to see your son. You can celebrate your birthdays together again. Heaven will be amazing." Peter and my dad shared the same birthdays. As I held him close, tears filled my eyes as I watched the graph of his heartbeat on the monitor turn into a flat line.

For my state of mind, his death proved to be the last straw.

After we buried my father and settled back into our routine, I spent the next two weeks searching for any kind of service to help me with Marston. There were none. I upped my Lord's Prayers and Hail Marys as well, but it was to no avail. I finally said to Eric, "I can't do this anymore. I know what's ahead." I started crying and then did what I did every night, as I tossed and turned and said the Lord's Prayer again and again, trusting only the sedative properties of repetition by that point. I could have just as easily been uttering the lyrics to "Row, Row, Row Your Boat" or "American Pie." My efforts were that futile, my faith that fragile.

There was one thing I still counted on in a world that was swimming in disappointment. Every morning, Eric would get up at five, shower, dress, come over to my side of the bed, put a hand on my shoulder, lean over, tenderly kiss me goodbye, and say, "I love you." Then, I'd feel my cheeks flush and respond with a sleepy smile before dozing back off. It was our moment of bliss.

On this particular morning, less than three weeks since my dad's death, life was no different. Eric rose with his alarm, which roused me, then I heard the shower go on and fell back to sleep. A bit later, I felt a hand on my shoulder. My eyes opened to slits like they always did. I found myself staring at a pair of really, really big feet on the floor. I instinctively knew these big feet by my bedside didn't belong to Eric. "What are you doing?" I asked.

The guy with the really big feet, my dad, who had stood at six feet five inches, responded, "You asked me to come."

Startled, I sat up. All I could feel was his energy around me. I was in the eye of a tornado of white light and energy. I could see him standing right there in front of me, but I felt him everywhere. He sat down on the bed, facing me.

"You can do this, Chrissy," he said, patting my leg. "Marston is going to be fine."

I wasn't scared, more in awe. It's difficult to explain or even comprehend, but his touch, his presence, and his scent, they were comforting and familiar. This brought me such peace.

In retrospect, I know this happened because my Lord's Prayers were a cry for help, and my Heavenly Father came to me in a form I would recognize—my dad—to remind me he would be there to guide me on this journey.

Then, a light came on from the closet and flooded the bedroom. I immediately turned toward it, and, when I looked back, my father was gone.

"Chris," Eric said. "What are you doing? Why are you sitting up?"

My heart was beating out of my chest. I was stunned and overwhelmed. I reached out and asked him to come over.

He did, and I pressed his hand to my heart, which was when I started crying and told him about the vision.

Eric called me every hour that day to check in.

You know how people say that even if things aren't so great in your life, you can be a miracle for someone else? There's a kid at the baseball field wearing worn-out shoes that are too small, and you have an extra pair of your kid's in the car. Someone in line at the grocery store is short, and you make up the difference. A hug at the right moment is a miracle to someone in need of physical comfort. A hug can change someone's life. And words, they have power. My father proved that to me that morning. He used his words to remind me of my own strength, as I had apparently forgotten about my mother and Paula and my role in everything. This was the miracle I'd needed.

Margaret, my oldest sister, said to me once, "I just wish you'd had the mother I did growing up, Chris. She was so incredible. She sparkled."

I had the mother that didn't get enough sleep, didn't have enough time for me, didn't have a lot of friends, wasn't up for shopping just for fun, and no longer went to the country club or the hair salon per protocol. My mother modeled what it meant to give care to a special needs child. My mother was a warrior, and I was her recruit. I was being prepared for a life with Marston since, well, forever. This meant I was already ready.

Shortly after my father came to me, Lorrie Weathers, my college roommate and one of my best friends, told me about her mother's experience with a child that was like Marston. Her mother, a teacher in South Florida, had a pupil that displayed symptoms of autism. The child's mother was taking her son to **The Institutes for the Achievement of Human Potential**, which was rumored to be revolutionary for kids "like ours." I loved Lorrie. I trusted her, and I felt like this was another sign from God that I was not to take lightly. Without hesitating, I called. They penciled me in for their first opening: December 8, 1998. They were booked eight months out.

Even that, though disappointing, gave me strength—eight months out? Wow.

This hope will sustain and carry me through the rest of summer and fall, I thought. *I just know it.*

My dedication to my son was about to spring to a new level, one I didn't even know I had in me.

"You got this, Chrissy. Marston is going to be just fine…."

5

THIS IS BAD

"A mother's love is the fuel that enables a normal human being to do the impossible."

—Marion C. Garretty

1998

I WORRIED NONSTOP ABOUT MARSTON'S mental capacity; he wasn't speaking well, and the gap between him and so-called normal children was increasing by the day. Marston was not catching up. The only constant was the rate at which he was falling behind. But, even in those dark days, I would see flashes of normalcy break through the storm clouds. These moments would give me hope that the Marston I knew was inside, was trying to get out.

I remember his older brothers, Austin and William, used to watch the *Three Stooges*. Marston would join them and be engaged and laugh at the appropriate times. He understood the gags, as well as the subtle humor, and would actually laugh out loud. A sense of humor is a higher brain function, something that requires reason, anticipation, reading one's environment, and understanding consequences.

Marston's nursery was close to our bedroom. We always checked on the kids before we went to sleep. However, even walking into Marston's room would cause him to sit straight up in bed. Austin could sleep through a hurricane. Every birthday, I would decorate Austin's room with banners and balloons while he was asleep; he never stirred. We always thought Marston could be in the CIA because of his ability to sense even small changes. He would be asleep with his door open, I would tiptoe in on the carpeted floor, not making a sound, and he would sit up out of a dead sleep and stare at me.

This ability, his canine sense of sound, soon translated into nighttime adventures. He would climb out of his crib and explore other places: the garage, the cars, the backyard. There was no cabinet that went unopened nor kitchen drawer left unexamined.

He became fascinated with keys. He'd take our key rings and, through observation only, pick out the right key for the right door or vehicle. Several times, we found him in the car, standing in the driver's seat, hands on the wheel with the key in the ignition. Unfortunately, this nightly routine made us feel like bad parents more than anything. We had a baby monitor, but Marston was so stealthy he never roused us. Out of safety concerns, we had to reverse his doorknob and lock him in at night. We didn't know what else to do, as he could unlock anything whether it required a key or not, rendering all "child safety" gadgets ineffective.

Brute measures aside, these abilities amazed me. They lit a fire under me to help him, and they kept it burning bright.

•°•°•°•

Was it the brush, the artist, the type of paints that created the ceiling of the Sistine Chapel? Is it genetics, practice, dedication, a little bit of luck that shape a world-class athlete? What about a successful relationship? Do Eric and I have a happy marriage because we're attracted to each other? Is it because we share the same religious beliefs? Do we parent similarly? Are we both football fans? Do we enjoy running, wine, sitcoms, reading thrillers, or watching the History Channel? Do we both enjoy seafood, modern art, helping local charities? Sometimes, it's impossible to tell why something is the way it is. Sometimes, you can't say, "This is the reason 'X' is working." Sometimes, we don't think about the whys; there are too many variables for one thing. Plus, no single "why" can be credited with the success of the painting, the athlete, the relationship. Most of the time, all these tiny, incremental changes don't feel or look like anything at all, and it's impossible to understand why something works.

When I say "nothing was helping my son," I mean I couldn't tell if it was helping him. It's not like I took him to speech therapy one day and he woke up reciting sonnets the next. I had nothing to gauge his progress by. I couldn't use Austin as a marker. I didn't know what progress looked like for Marston. I didn't have an MRI or ultrasound that could look inside his brain and track what was happening. So, were my efforts in vain? It felt like it most days, but I kept going.

I talked ceaselessly. That was one of my tactics. Marston couldn't really verbalize any of his needs, so, to be honest, I didn't really know what was "going in" when I chatted up a storm (daily). But, I figured if I just kept talking, maybe someday it would all click. We'd be driving somewhere, and I'd point to a fire truck and go into as much simple detail as I could. We'd be grocery shopping, and I'd show him all the different fruits and vegetables and talk about their color, taste, if they grow in the ground or hang from a tree, etc. The sky, the beach, the rain, the moon—just like with any child, you want them to learn about the whole wide world. With Marston, I was on steroids about it, and I was repetitive, too. But he seemed to enjoy it, or at least not mind me talking all day long.

Marston never really had any moods or mood swings, and he's never had a bad day in his life, except for the short stint we had with Adderall the fall of 1998.

I went and saw a psychiatrist, maybe because waiting around for the winter appointment with the Institute for the Achievement of Human Potential proved harder than I thought, maybe because we hadn't tried this type of medical professional. Several people tossed around the acronym ADD; that was gaining popularity faster than autism. I figured it couldn't hurt, so I made appointment with a new doctor. He recommended Adderall. "It'll help him focus," he said.

He's not unfocused, but okay....

We tried several different dosages over the course of a month. We may have switched brand names, too, but I don't recall. Marston cried on this drug. All the time. I'd give him the meds, and, within a couple hours, he'd be fidgeting uncomfortably, or he'd lie on the floor, sobbing. He literally fell to the ground in the middle of grocery shopping one day.

"What's wrong, Marston?" I asked.

He shook his head. "I...don't...."

He didn't know. It was the drugs. He'd been invaded, and they made him excessively emotional, downright miserable. They changed his personality. Marston was a content kid. He looks like me but acts like his father, and his dad is an easygoing, cool guy who's calm during any given situation and just plain comfortable in his own skin. Marston was born with that same laid-back attitude. Austin is more like me. He wants to get things right the first time. When he's stumped, he wants the answer yesterday. He's a perfectionist. Friendly, yes, we're all really friendly, but Marston and

Eric are my easygoing men. But on the ADD meds? It was a disaster.

I can honestly say that was the worst month of his life.

Additionally, I saw no improvements on the pills. I'm not suggesting they don't work for ADD; they just didn't work for Marston. So, we stopped them. It was easy to ween him, as he hadn't been on them very long. After that, we went back to playing the waiting game.

Marston's happy-go-lucky disposition didn't trump the loneliness and isolation of autism. (It probably helped ease the pain in our hearts more than anything.) When Marston wanted to join in with the other kids, like with Austin and his friends when he saw them speaking so freely and easily, he'd stare at me with wonder. I knew what he was thinking. *Why can't I do that?* But, then, he'd go off on his own and find one of his favorite toys, generally something plastic or metal and angular, and he'd be content again. That's about as bad as his moods ever got. He'd want his sippy cup. It was within reach, but he'd think and think and then drag his high chair to the cup. That was his signal: *I'm thirsty.* The sippy was associated with the high chair (from when he was really little), so when he put them together, in his mind, it created clarity.

Colors and numbers: I went bananas with that! I'd say, "Go put on your purple pajamas." And he'd run to his room and come back wearing his purple pajamas. "What color are your pajamas, Marston?" I'd then ask. And he'd just stare at me with wonder.

I believe everything I did and continue to do (to date) is benefitting him in small ways that I'm not necessarily meant to see or understand. And all the therapies, classes, treatments—they were benefitting me, too.

At the beginning of my *"this is bad"* epiphany, I ended every day exhausted, as I'd spent all my time either physically working to help my son or researching and reading everything I could, hoping for answers. As a result, I started sleeping better. Helpless is a horrible feeling, so keeping busy sure got me out of my own head. Marston and I had to keep moving and keep trying. Initially, that brought me great comfort.

6

THIS PROGRAM IS NO JOKE

"The brain is a monstrous, beautiful mess."

—Susannah Cahalan
Brain on Fire: My Month of Madness

THE INSTITUTES FOR THE ACHIEVEMENT of Human Potential, the place we waited eight months to get into—*to get an initial meeting*—is not one of those programs that strives for micro miracles. This place had the most difficult program of anything I've ever done in my life. When you google The Institutes, you'll see mixed reviews. From my research, everyone who has ever committed to the program raves about it. The negativity or skepticism written about The Institutes comes from (outside) medical professionals who disagree with the philosophy and from parents who didn't actually invest in the program due to the intense financial and time commitment required. For starters, if you enroll in IAHP, it's mandatory that either mom or dad be a stay-at-home parent. The schedule they put you and your child on is that rigorous. For this reason, many people don't make it past the initial meeting—*the meeting they waited nearly a year to attend.*

I went into that meeting with a pen in one hand and my checkbook in the other. I was a mom with nothing to lose. This meant we were game, and I wasn't leaving without a start date in writing.

•°•°•°•

The Institutes for the Achievement of Human Potential was established in 1955 by Glenn Doman. Glenn is deceased now, but I met with Glenn, and he met and evaluated Marston. He tried to meet with everyone who was a part of his program.

> The Institutes is internationally known for its pioneering work in child brain development. The objective of The Institutes is to help all children achieve intellectual, physical and social excellence—to help brain-injured children achieve wellness and well children achieve excellence.
>
> Their philosophy is straightforward:
> There is nothing more important in the life of the **brain-injured** child than seeing that child get better every day. It is often said that there are no 'cures' for brain injury and, of course, this is true. The word 'cure' is not appropriate in the

context of brain injury. For the vast majority of children, brain injury is not a progressive disease, but instead the incident that caused the injury is over and what is left is a good brain that has gotten hurt and needs help.

Our job is to take each child no matter how injured the brain may be and to move that child to the highest level of function that our present knowledge of brain growth and development will permit.

The objective of The Institutes is to take special needs children and help them to achieve normality physically, intellectually, physiologically and socially.

The majority of children achieve one of these goals, and many children achieve two of these goals. Some children achieve all of these goals, and some children achieve none of these goals.

Founder Glenn Doman believed in both mending and exercising the brain—however injured—to unleash its full potential. He disagreed with the philosophy that very young children (babies) were incapable of learning in large capacities. For this reason, The Institutes caters to all ages, newborns through adulthood.

Glenn was a war hero before devoting his life to serving severely brain-injured children across the globe. It has been said that "he drove mothers and babies closer together." To this, Glenn has responded, "Put that on my tombstone and I will rest well."

Historically, children diagnosed with developmental delay, cerebral palsy, autism, Trisomy 21 (Down syndrome), Attention Deficit Disorder, hyperactivity, learning problems, dyslexia and a host of other symptomatic diagnoses have been considered hopeless.

Profoundly brain-injured children may be blind, deaf, insensate, paralyzed or speechless. They may have significant problems with food absorption, respiration and even survival. They may have all these problems. Severely brain-injured children may have serious visual, auditory, tactile, mobility, speech or manual problems. They may have all these problems.

Moderately brain-injured children may have significant problems in one or all of the sensory and motor pathways. Mildly brain-injured children may have reading, learning, behavior, balance, coordination, speech or writing problems. They may have all these problems.

Most of these special needs children will have significant health issues ranging from failure to thrive, to chronic upper respiratory illness, reflux, asthma, nutritional problems, food intolerance and allergies. The brain-injured children admitted to The Institutes programs range in age from newborn to adults. No child or adult is ever refused admission to the program because of the severity of his or her brain injury.

Hundreds of thousands of parents have come to The Institutes to learn how to help their children at home. Those parents have proven beyond any doubt that brain-injured children are not hopeless, but instead have tremendous potential. The Institutes exists to ensure that all brain-injured children have a fighting chance to be well.

The Institutes believes there is no stronger influence on a young mind than that of a parent:

Parents who have been carefully instructed in **early intelligence development** are the very best teachers for their own children.

All children love to learn...the younger a child is, the easier it is for the child to learn.

The parent and child together are the most dynamic teaching and learning team. The family is the cradle for intellectual, physical, and social excellence in the child.

The objective of The Institutes is to make children intellectually, physically, and socially excellent.

The first thing that happens upon admittance is a folder is created for your child called **The Institutes Developmental Profile™**.

When The Institutes began there was no reliable evaluation procedure for hurt or brain-injured children. Glenn Doman and the staff developed the first reliable set of procedures to evaluate children with neurological problems.

The Institutes Developmental Profile™ measures the growth and development of the brain. This profile allows us to evaluate a child and make an exact comparison between the hurt child and his well peers. This provides an accurate rate of growth for the child and establishes a baseline against which each child can be evaluated to determine his progress.

Each time a child returns to The Institutes, a new developmental profile is done and a new program is created based upon that profile.

This was music to my ears. Finally, professionals in the field of neurological disorders and brain injury were able to look inside Marston's mind. We were going to track his progress and grade him (for lack of a better word) as we worked through the regiment.

From December 1998 to 2004, Marston and I committed to IAHP with the hope of upping his psychological, intellectual, and physical well-being. There are dozens of programs to suit your child's needs at The Institutes. After our evaluation, which took four to five days, the staff, Eric, and I agreed the following classes were the most critical.

1. The Nutrition Program—while hard for many, my dietician training made this logical and easy. I was already doing most of it.

2. The Physical Excellence Program—recreating/resetting brainstem function
   a. Patterning
   b. Creeping
   c. Crawling
   d. Brachiation

3. How to Teach Your Baby to Read Program

4. How to Teach Your Baby Mathematics Program

5. Oxygen Masking Program

The first thing I had to do was get through the courses designed to teach parents how to implement these classes at home. (This is why there needs to be a stay-at-home parent.) I enrolled in all of the above. After six weeks of training and working with Marston during that time, I was on my own, with incremental updates, conferences, and biannual visits to The Institutes to monitor his progress.

Physical Activity

Masking: we did this ninety (yes, 90) times a day in one-minute intervals. Initially, he was breathing a gas high in CO_2 as well as oxygen. Most people don't know the stimulus to breathe is not the lack of oxygen but the buildup of CO_2. Carbon dioxide is a powerful cerebral vasodilator. Dilation, the buildup of CO_2, also increases blood flow to the brain by dilating the arteries. Breathing in this gaseous mixture, along with the dilation, forces one's system to instinctually breathe deep and fast, causing hyperventilation generally in under a minute. Therefore, the brain gets more oxygen from the rapid and deep breathing. This also develops the chest wall muscles and diaphragm, just like pushups develop the pectoral muscles.

I had been regretting that Marston hadn't stayed on oxygen for the full first year of his life, and now, here we were using it as an alternative medicine to help heal his brain. By the way, ninety times a day means masking over seven times an hour for twelve hours every day. We did this for years.

He eventually graduated to a **rebreathing mask**, which was much simpler than the mask he'd used initially. This increased the CO_2 in his respirations because he was exhaling into the mask and then "rebreathing" that CO_2 back in. (Remember: CO_2 is the cerebral vasodilator—it increases blood flow to the brain.) With this process, he would hyperventilate, which was the goal. Since you are not breathing in air, but a gas rich in carbon dioxide, the levels of carbon dioxide inside your body never get to drop. You keep breathing in more and more. This pushes the oxygen in your bloodstream to the needed tissue, and it strengthens the muscles of respiration to increase lung capacity over time. **More carbon dioxide in the body requires more oxygen to create balance**. Marathon runners, or anybody playing an endurance sport, like basketball or soccer, build their cardio strength by conditioning their heart and lungs during practices. This is what rebreathing does, and it does it faster (in a matter of minutes).

This additional "gas" in the bloodstream gives the lungs, muscles, brain, and body in general the ability to grow, and therefore to exercise beyond its regular capacity.

Within three months, amazing healing had occurred. Marston's chest wall circumference—a measure of lung capacity and chest wall musculature—went from below the second percentile to the ninetieth percentile. He was now getting enough oxygen to fuel even more healing. (This measurement is determined by subtracting the difference between a fully-exhaled chest circumference from the measurement after a full inhalation.)

We worked on **patterning** daily. Marston loved this. He just lay there, relaxed, while we manipulated his extremities gently, creating cross-body patterns.

Patterning involves placing a child in prone (tummy position) over a treatment table. Alternately, a standard rectangular dinner table may be used. Patterning utilizes the principle of moving the head, arms, and legs in a reciprocal swimming motion or 'patterning' range of movement. Patterning, when viewed by the casual observer, appears as if three adults are working with a child to assist him with crawling in place. However, it is important to remember that Patterning must always be performed in a structured manner using safe biomechanical movement techniques and only with trained personnel.

Patterning was developed by Glenn Doman. The goal is to improve gross and fine motor skills by influencing the brain through passive movements. Phylogenetic development is the set of scientific stages of development and evolution in a species from infancy to adulthood—the patterns it follows. With brain-injured children, the goal with patterning is to complete each stage (or "said" stage) of development that was skipped or not reached…and then move on to the next, and so on. I performed the patterning exercises on Marston eight times a day in five-minute increments.

We turned this into a fun family event, with the first therapy session early in the morning, before Eric left for work. The second session was scheduled for right before the older boys left for school. I had friends come over every couple of hours during the day to help. Then, I'd finish up the protocol with the boys after school, and the eighth and final daily session happened after Eric came home. We played music and sang to Marston to keep these exercises lively and fun.

We had to crawl 400 meters a day and creep one mile a day (1,600 meters). In the world of physical therapy, **crawling** happens when your stomach is touching the ground. I guess you could say you look a bit like a crab when you crawl. Maybe you've seen military people doing it during drills, when they crawl under ropes and look like they're almost flat on the ground. **Creeping** is on all fours, with the stomach off the ground (what most parents call crawling). The importance of creeping and crawling has been well-documented. Left- and right-brain coordination is enhanced by creeping, crawling, jumping jacks, and other cross-body exercises that stimulate both sides of the brain simultaneously. Creeping and crawling force the brain to communicate across the midline. This skill is needed for reading to occur. That is how important it is. This is not to say your child can't grow up with normal and healthy brain function if they skip crawling, but, if there are any noticeable issues, this is a good first place to look. Again, Marston did this without complaint.

As the protocol expanded and we needed to creep and crawl longer distances, Eric would take him to the beach and they would exercise in the sand. Many times, this happened in the darkness of the early morning, before Eric went to work. I was busy getting Austin breakfast and off to school. I often wondered what my friends and neighbors thought of our crazy and obsessive early-morning rituals.

Running. We had to run (another cross-body activity) over a mile a day. And I do mean "we." He was a toddler, so if he was running, I was running. We broke the running into seventy sprints of twenty-five yards and spread that throughout our waking hours. Once Marston had the endurance, Eric started taking over this task at four a.m. daily. He'd wake Marston for round one, go to the beach, and they'd run for a mile. Then, they'd come home, Eric would shower, get ready for work, and then we would fit in a patterning session before Eric left for work. The boys and I would get two more patterning sessions in before school.

Brachiation is the final exercise in the Physical Excellence Program that we worked on daily. The definition of brachiation is arm swinging, which translated to playing on the monkey bars for most of us. It does the obvious: develop upper-body strength, balance, and coordination. Physical development stimulates brain development and learning capabilities, which is the big-picture reason why it's an important exercise.

There is also a…

…potential capacity for brachiation to be a robust stimulus to both the nervous and neuroendocrine systems…to produce a very centering, calming, and organizing down-regulation of a body subjected to stressful circumstances [a brain injury]. This train of thought suggests that applications of different types of movement patterns [like arm swinging] may have implications that go well beyond the ways that we generally think of them.

Because brachiation requires a lot of strength and coordination, it's harder to teach to a child that isn't "traditionally" reachable, like a child with autism. This was challenging for a number of reasons. Physically, it didn't seem to be a natural movement for Marston. Intellectually, he didn't really "get it." Logistically speaking, we didn't live next to a park. Eric had a friend who was a carpenter and adored Marston. On learning about Marston's new program, he drew up a plan, went to Home Depot, and, in a few days, we had a set of "monkey bars" in our backyard. We would hold Marston by the waist and coach him to swing his body and move his arms along the bars—another cross-body, cross-brain activity.

In between masking, creeping, crawling, patterning, running, and brachiation, we kept plenty busy.

Academics

The reading and mathematics programs were as rigorous as the physical activity program. The IAHP, as you can imagine, also provided us with great and unique ways to teach math and reading. We created books and special flashcards to help Marston learn words, numbers, and how to read simple sentences. During the time we were enrolled in IAHP, they also had a list of facts they wanted all their students to memorize and store. They called these facts "bits of intelligence." These were bits of information that could be stored in the brain for later use (later reference in life). These included the names of flowers, birds, animals, painters, inventors, composers, dinosaurs, cities, etc. Along with the word on the front came three bits of intelligence on the back.

If, for example, the front of the flashcard had *dinosaur* on it, the back would say:

- *The word "dinosaur" means "terrible lizard."*
- *Dinosaurs were reptiles.*
- *Most dinosaurs were not giant, but the size of the average human.*

Front of flashcard: *Vincent van Gogh*
Back of flashcard:

- *He had a brother who was also named Vincent van Gogh.*
- *He sold only one painting in his lifetime.*
- *He cut off his ear and mailed it to the woman he loved.*

Front of flashcard: *Mount Rushmore*
Back of flashcard:

- *The sculpture took fourteen years to complete.*
- *George Washington's face is sixty feet long.*
- *Dynamite was used to carve most of the heads.*

The other exercise we did with reading required building our own storybooks. And, when I say storybooks, I mean we built over 100 cardboard books. The idea here was to create stories with Marston as the main character to help connect him to words, sentences, and story structure. I would write a simple book about Marston being a fireman and saving a cat from a tree. Marston would be a football player and make the pass for a winning touchdown. Marston was an astronaut landing on the moon. Jett was the name of our dog at the time. Marston loved books about Jett. Eventually, Jett would start starring in the books, too. At the end of these storybooks, there'd be a pocket with eight words from the story stuffed inside. We'd then go over those words.

What was happening in the mind of my son with all these flashcards, storybooks, and bits of intelligence? Great question.

When Marston was around ten, our efforts came full circle. We were at the National Gallery of Art in Washington, DC, and he pointed to one of van Gogh's paintings and said, "That man cut off his ear." In that moment, I felt pure joy for Marston and us as a family. It was a reminder that no effort is ever wasted, even if you do not see the results immediately.

Nutrition

The first thing they tell you at The Institutes in regard to your child's nutritional needs and well-being is that dairy products

are harmful. If you do no other thing, please eliminate dairy from your child's diet. This was gospel.

> Cow's milk contains casein, which reacts with the opiate receptors in the temporal lobes of the brain. The temporal lobes are involved with speech and auditory integration. When casein reacts with the opiate receptors in the temporal lobes, it can mimic the effect of opiate drugs, and this may negatively impact speech and auditory integration. It is worth noting that the peptide from milk is called casomorphin.

The Institutes understands we've been conditioned to feed our children cow's milk and other dairy products and that this is not an easy change for some people. To this, they've said:

> Mothers are afraid to stop dairy products. Secretly, we think something terrible will happen if we stop dairy products. It's not true. Something good will happen. That runny nose will stop running. Those chronic ear infections will disappear. Those black circles under your child's eyes will go away and not come back. The trips to the doctor, or worse, the hospital, will become fewer. Appetite, sleep and behavior— all may be much better. For some children, understanding and language will improve as well.

The Institutes recommend tracking six weeks in the life of your child without dairy and documenting the changes. Green, leafy vegetables, beans, seeds, wild salmon, and sardines all provide calcium. They don't recommend soy products, as they've discovered through trial and error that many kids react adversely to soy. Many degenerative diseases adults suffer and die from are caused from a lifetime of poor eating habits, including cardiovascular disease, kidney disease, type II diabetes, obesity. Inflammation has been affiliated with poor diet and dairy products. Inflammation is a common symptom for people suffering from autoimmune and a myriad of other diseases and chronic ailments.

Their second nutritional tip: don't feed your child the same thing every day. Mothers seem to cater to the dictates of their child when they should be introducing a wide variety of tastes and healthy choices for optimum health.

Don't blend food. Blending exposes food to the air, and it immediately starts losing its nutritional value.

Don't "batch" food. Don't make so much food that you can survive on it all week or freeze it for the future. Having enough leftovers for breakfast or lunch the next day is fine. But, food loses all nutritional value shortly after it is cooked; it needs to be eaten.

Slow cooking lentils and beans ensures they are fully cooked. Pressure cooking does not. It's important to cook food enough so that it can be readily digested, the nutrients absorbed, and waste eliminated with ease. But, overcooking leads to loss of nutrition in the vegetable before ingestion.

The Institutes always recommends steaming your vegetables separately and not cooking them in with your meats. Rotating your grains (feeding with variety) keeps nutritional intake at its highest. Some grains The Institutes recommends are brown rice, buckwheat, amaranth, millet, and quinoa. Avoid wheat because so many children are reactive to it.

The whole family went on Marston's nutritional food program. In our case, there was very little change evident, as I had the whole family eating "healthy" from the get-go. As I mentioned earlier, my college major was food and nutrition, and my minor was chemistry. I was fully aware of the nutritional issues associated with milk products, gluten, and processed food. This was under control from the beginning.

We adhered to the program, and all the classes in which we were enrolled, to the letter.

The people at The Institutes were amazing. They were the first professionals to understand not only Marston, but also my need to help him. They gave us hope. We saw other parents making progress with brain issues, too, ranging from trauma to Down syndrome throughout the five to six years we were involved. We'd connect at follow-up evaluations when we'd fly in and exchange information, so we could stay in touch and monitor our children's progress collectively. Semi-annual conferences also proved to be great places to network. This was the first real taste I got of the importance of having not just a team of doctors, but a team of moms, too.

This is not an easy program, and not everybody can do it. We ran from one "event" to the next every day, over and over. We started at (or before, in Eric's case) the crack of dawn, and we were exhausted beyond belief by mid-evening. (It took us well into every evening to complete the daily list of tasks). The repetitive nature of the activities had as much to do with our exhaustion as the long work days. In fact, a lot of the criticism from both pediatricians and parents is about the program being "impossible to implement," particularly with any kind of regularity. Parents feel bad when they can't maintain the protocol—this has been the main complaint over the years.

We committed for over five years, despite the logistical challenges, and feel that it was an enormous benefit to Marston.

We believe his capacity to learn, his capability to function in society, his ability to communicate effectively, and his lack of debilitating sensory issues are direct results of early intervention from the IAHP.

The Institutes Developmental Profile was revisited every few months to gauge his progress. Each student and their designated parent were given a mentor/coach; we reported to them. Once you got the programs down (each program is tailor-made for each child), it became the language with which to gauge progress. I'd call in—unless we flew there to meet in person, which happened at least three times a year—and the meeting would go something like this: "Marston successfully creeps X distance in X amount of time (or X times daily). He started running one mile in twenty-three minutes, and now, he can run one mile in seventeen minutes." Then, our coach would say something like: "Sounds great. Let's stop with the creeping altogether and graduate to two miles a day running." Then, we'd talk about the masking. I had his "before and after" chest measurements—it was the first sign of progress I'd seen in Marston since birth, him increasing his capacity to take in oxygen and building the muscles in his lungs. He graduated successfully from five breathing treatments per hour to one treatment per hour. After two months of that, he graduated to a type of breathing treatment that involved an oxygen tank, followed by masking. Once your brain-injured child graduates to another level, it would be odd to regress. The brain or body has learned to manage a new skill. It becomes involuntary, as that part of the injured brain is now considered healed. This is the phylogenetic development I was talking about earlier.

From 1999 through 2004, his progress was remarkable.

Most of what I considered progress for Marston might not have been visible to people who didn't really know him, which is important to understand.

- Within a year of being in the program, his gait became normal. There had always been something peculiar or cumbersome in his style of walking and in his mannerisms. He looked like he was working harder than everyone else. That vanished. He walks and moves normally now.

- His sensory issues had disappeared entirely by the time we left IAHP.

- It was no longer challenging or distracting for Marston to be around people in a classroom environment or a crowd.

- At first glance, his speech was what had (and has always) set him apart from other kids. So, it stood to reason that his speech would be the last thing to kick in during all our years with The Institutes. And it was. But, while we were waiting on that, his comprehension skills went through the roof. You could see in his eyes that he was "getting it." He was beginning to understand everything, even though he still couldn't respond effectively.

Marston's brain wasn't capable of processing how to create complete sentences. And, integrating the use of articles into his everyday vocabulary seemed like something he might never be able to do. If you've ever studied a foreign language intensively and over a long period of time and then gone to that country to discover you can understand it but not speak it, you know what I mean. Marston was starting to be able to understand language and communication, even though he couldn't fold himself into individual or group discussions. He couldn't read, either. I think he recognized the shape of certain words, but the letters themselves held no meaning. But the progress he'd made with gross motor skill development, sensory processing, focus, and comprehension was undeniable.

.°.°.°.

One night, about four years into the IAHP program—I think it was around the time Marston was seven—I would see the results of this intensive program in action.

We were praying in bed, like usual, when Marston asked God for Austin's brain. He said it, of course, in his way, but I understood him perfectly. It was a dagger to my heart. I told him, "Your brain is perfect, sweetheart. God doesn't make mistakes. Austin has these certain sets of talents—he's a great communicator, math comes easy to him, he's great at sports—but everyone is different, Marston. God made you sweet and gave you a beautiful smile. He knows what he's doing, and we have to trust him."

Moving past the heartbreak, I realized this was a huge breakthrough. He recognized Austin's unique abilities, and he was differentiating them from his own.

This is comprehension.

7

SOCIALIZATION DOES MATTER

"Never give up on anybody. Miracles happen every day."

—H. Jackson Brown Jr.
Life's Little Instruction Book

2000

BY THE TIME MARSTON WAS five—we'd been with the IAHP for just over a year—I was gaining on this disorder in enough small ways that I felt he should be around other kids.

Autistic kids often don't display a need to play with others. Does that mean they don't want to be included? Or, do they just not have the language skills to integrate themselves? I didn't know for sure, but I pray on everything, and I prayed on this, too, asking for direction. Having done that, and after having numerous conversations with Eric, we looked into a local Montessori school and enrolled him. By this point, the amount of time we had to spend patterning, creeping, crawling, and masking was decreasing, and life was more manageable. This made it possible for Marston to spend two or three mornings a week, from nine to noon, at the Montessori school and still integrate all the protocols from The Institutes.

He was delayed compared to the other five-year-olds but looked right in a classroom full of kids. He could sit still and focus on things he liked, such as puzzles, picture books, and beads. And, he never bothered the other kids. His teacher, a saint, seemed excited to have him, to help him, and to help us move forward in our son's education.

From age three to age six is when children learn how to interact with other children and adults. They learn the ground rules of socialization and living successfully in society. This is essential for proper brain development. Understanding reward and punishment, how to share, how to interact within a group setting in general, how to express wants and needs, how to interpret the wants and needs of others, as well as learning basic rights from wrongs and feeling secure in social settings—these are all things that develop in the healthy brains of our young children before they get to the first grade.

Montessori schools specialize in independent learning and believe every child should be able to work at their own pace, but in an environment that cultivates interaction, as well, because of the brain's great capacity for learning and its need for socialization. Even though Marston couldn't communicate like his peers, we all thought this was the right place for him to establish some of these skills.

Everything that happens with our physical bodies (from sneezing to scratching an itch to talking to throwing a ball) stems from proper brain development. Linguists say that babies are born with grammatical tools and learn language as if it is instinctual just from being exposed to people who are communicating verbally. Gross- and fine-motor-skill development stem from healthy brain development. From as early as two and three months old, the healthy brain of an infant understands the point of smiling and crying to satisfy immediate needs and interact with the world around them. Short- and long-term memory are being developed prior to the first year of life. A clear understanding of right and wrong is being fashioned in the healthy brain of a two-year-old. By the time a child is three or four, they are learning how to label their emotions, and emotional intelligence (EQ or EI) is forming. Of course, emotional intelligence does not exist in isolation from other kinds of intelligence; they go hand in hand. Children that are emotionally competent tend to perform better in school. While math and science activities are important to academic success, activities that allow children to explore their emotions and sense of self are also important to their development. What some people don't know is that emotions can do a lot to influence how strongly we remember details and events and retain information. It's impossible to exercise and develop emotional intelligence without being around another person and groups of people. The development of EQ must go beyond the parent-child bond to evolve fully. And, emotional intelligence and understanding socialization, like learning to ride a bike, happen through repetition—practice.

I want to explain briefly how this kind of repetition happens at the cellular level. There are these tiny gaps connecting the nerve endings in our brain called synapses. The space (like a hallway) at the end of one neuron allows a signal to pass from it to the neuron next to it. Through repetition, these connections (synapses) are made stronger. Synapses are vital to healthy brain function, especially when it comes to memory. I'm not referring to memory as in memorizing a poem; I'm talking about memory that is used for language or understanding emotions. These kinds of memories are near-impossible to "break" or undo once the link in the brain is formed.

When a nerve signal reaches the end of the neuron, it cannot simply continue to the next cell. Instead, it must trigger the release of neurotransmitters. Neurotransmitters (these are chemical messengers) get dumped into the synapse (the hallway) in what are called vesicles (tiny sacs) and travel through the synapse to the next neuron, where they bind (or are "picked up" by receptors). This triggers the action or change that the initial neuron is requesting. These actions can be voluntary (waving to a friend) or involuntary (breathing). Billions of neurotransmitter molecules work nonstop to keep our brains functioning, managing everything in our bodies.

Neurotransmitters may excite the neuron they bind to or inhibit it when the receptors take this information in and perform the action (or, again, inhibit the action).

Early in a child's life, their brain will start to form synapses at a faster rate than at any other time in life. They're actually producing many more than they need, and not all of them will make it to adulthood. This allows children to learn things more quickly than adults do. This is simple math.

Anyone with kids knows that genetics plays a role. Kids come with their own personalities, but brain development can be heavily influenced by external factors, as well. What we understand about nature vs. nurture is that the genes fuel this mass synapse formation, but the environment fine-tunes the brain and helps it make decisions about which pathways to keep and which to get rid of. The more often a synapse is used, or the more often a skill or idea is practiced or heard, the stronger that synapse gets. This means things that are used often, like language and walking, stay ingrained in a child's brain, while things that are neglected disappear. This process also happens in the brains of adults, but at a much slower rate.

Because your baby is rapidly creating synapses, this is a critical period for learning things. It also means that without practice, certain skills will disappear, because, just as they are creating synapses, their brains are pruning (literally getting rid of) the synapses that are not being used. If you want to create lasting skills in your child (like learning a second language, a musical instrument, even manners) it's imperative that their exposure and practice is constant. Children's "flexible" brains provide a unique opportunity to create a solid foundation on which to build for the rest of their lives.

Marston needed to be around other kids. It was time.

Up to this point, he had been a single student among rotating teachers. Eric and I knew that the window in his brain was open to create synapses pertaining to emotional connections. Yes, we knew he couldn't actually interact like other children, but, in the hopes of exercising and ultimately healing his injured brain, it seemed crucial he be submersed in an environment where language and emotional intelligence were being practiced all around him.

We hired a classroom assistant, CJ, to shadow Marston during the mornings at Montessori Tides, and we started speech therapy again with Nancy Lotowitz. (She worked with Marston for twelve years total). After school, we hired his teacher, Mrs. Dottie, to help him keep up with the class lessons. Oftentimes, he didn't understand how to begin some of the art projects, and self-learning didn't come easy. He needed help to understand the "Montessori way" of learning.

Mrs. Dottie was incredible. She loved Marston and had so much patience. Her skillset was inspiring. As much education as I'd had at that point, I wasn't a teacher certified in special needs. It was delightful to watch her interact with Marston. And the other kids in the classroom were accepting of Marston without question. (He was the only student with special needs.) At that age, kids don't look for differences, don't lead with their egos, and don't hate. Still, he wasn't asked to anyone's home for a playdate or invited to birthday parties. Due to his limited ability to communicate back, I imagine he came off as uninterested in most classroom activities, and in individual classmates, too. It was obvious to me, however, how happy he was to be part of that type of environment. I could gauge his various levels of contentment by that point, and being around his peers made him very happy.

In 2001, Mrs. Dottie left her part-time position at **Montessori Tides** for a full-time position at **Montessori Discovery**. The new Montessori school was for kindergarten through fifth grade. Class time ran from 8:30 a.m. to 3:00 p.m. The philosophy of allowing children to find their own rhythm when learning and to discover their own personal interests—with the idea that those will then be cultivated—seemed like a perfect next step for Marston. But, we couldn't stay enrolled in IAHP and send Marston off with regular kids that went to school all day long. We'd never be able to pull off both curriculums; there wasn't enough time in each day.

As an involved parent, you are constantly monitoring your child. Sometimes, it's necessary to explore new schools, activities, and therapies that could be beneficial. After five years of IAHP, and after tremendous growth, Marston had begun to plateau in his behavior. He began to express a desire for more socialization.

We decided to change course. We are forever grateful to Glenn Doman and the IAHP staff for helping us on our journey. He was a giant.

The decision did not come easy, but we followed Mrs. Dottie and enrolled Marston in Montessori Discovery, with speech therapy, physical therapy, and occupational therapy treatments after school.

This school was more regimented than Montessori Tides in its daily schedule, as the kids were older. The majority of them were capable of more rules and more rigor, and they even thrived on it. Marston was six and a half years old and placed in Mrs. Dottie's kindergarten class. This (his older age), coupled with the small class size experience (there were under 200 kids in the whole school, rendering less than twenty kids per class), as well as CJ assisting Marston, made us feel confident that he would get the attention he needed.

He did for the first year. It was wonderful. Mrs. Dottie, who'd become a close friend of the family by then, gave us bi-weekly, if not daily, reports. Marston had a real connection with her. Mrs. Dottie exuded kindness, patience, and compassion, and her energy was magnetic. Marston knew he was safe around her, knew she loved him.

He began to understand the rules of the classroom, too. He understood the regimen of the day, the structure/routine, and was comforted by its predictability. I volunteered three days a week in the classroom, and it was exciting to watch him catch on and follow suit like the other kids.

My allegiance with IAHP and the ideology of the Montessori schools was immense—but they just weren't enough to satisfy my need to heal Marston's injured brain and educate him to the full extent of what I believed he was capable. I needed a circle of moms with kids like Marston. I knew they'd be my best source of information. Plus, I had a lot to offer to them by that point, too.

8

STRONGER TOGETHER

"It is literally true that you can succeed best and quickest by helping others to succeed."

—Napoleon Hill
Think and Grow Rich

THERE WAS STILL NO FACEBOOK, no easy access to everything. I could feel the worldwide network of communication evolving, though, especially as someone who had been immersed in research and obsessed with "finding answers" since Marston's birth in 1995. I knew having answers at my fingertips was on the horizon. The days of selling encyclopedias door to door were over, but my "now," back then in the early 2000s, fell somewhere between these two extremes. We had the web, but not the kind of networking there is now. What I did have back then was a little extra time, with Marston having a longer school day.

So, without there being such a thing as a Facebook page to "like" or forums to join, I had to resort to *actual* over *virtual* reality to create the group I was envisioning. *Where are my warrior moms?* This was my next mission.

They were in my hometown, right in my backyard.

There were many women who lived locally with special needs kids. (I would come to discover that my original warrior moms all had children who displayed characteristics that would one day be described on the autistic spectrum.)

We started meeting to exchange stories, information, therapies, and to look for conferences to attend so we could accumulate more information. (One of these moms, Leslie Weed, would go on to create HEAL [Helping Enrich Autistic Life], a great foundation that has raised millions of dollars and given back to our community since January 2007. I am proud to call her a friend.)

We started looking for doctors who were doing research in fields that involved brain diseases and disorders—strokes, Alzheimer's, traumatic brain injury, MS, cancer, neurological disorders. We read everything we could find.

If there was a medical conference nearby, I'd attend it with another mom or two, or go alone if I had to. If I wasn't allowed to attend, because I was not a medical professional, I'd still find a way to go or have someone attend for me. Once, when I was driving alone, I caught myself singing along to *Barney* an hour into the trip.

Here are some of the therapies and treatments that were discovered and implemented because of my warrior moms' group:

Tomatis® therapy. I believed this was pivotal in helping Marston from ages five through eight.

The **Tomatis® Method** uses unanticipated sound contrasts through music and vocal intonations in order to constantly surprise the brain. That element of surprise forces the brain to develop automatic mechanisms to detect change, which ultimately serves to develop stronger focus and attention.

The fundamental principle of the Tomatis Method is that any influence on the mechanisms of reception and analysis of an acoustic message will affect the way in which this message is reproduced.

The brain tends to protect itself naturally by filtering the analysis of sensory information. It especially happens when the external environment is perceived as threatening or after an emotional shock. By stimulating the vast network of nerves that controls the overall level of brain activity, the Tomatis Method has positive effects on the control of emotion, as well as on the regulation of stress.

The most important organ in the ear associated with balance, movement, and coordination is called the vestibular nerve. The Tomatis Method, through its direct interaction with the vestibular nerve, has an effect on the regulation of muscle tone, both vertically and laterally. The vestibular nerve, in association with several other parts of the brain, plays an important role in the coordination and rhythm mechanisms.

The Tomatis Method stimulates the neural circuits linking the ear to the brain, creating what we call "mirror neurons." The mirror neuron system plays an important role in social interaction, cognition, and communication. The Tomatis Method is a complementary approach, which is often used in conjunction with other therapies and programs to help those on the autism spectrum.

We discovered a Dr. Stanley Greenspan in Washington, DC. He had a program called **Affect-Based Language Curriculum**. Marston was enrolled in that from 2002–2006. An online version of these programs started in 2010, and we enrolled in those, too.

The Hill Academic Center was a place where parents and teachers could go and get training to teach their special needs kids how to read. The program was called **Ready Program Methodology & Math**. Marston attended a six-week summer program in July 2005.

Another intervention program we signed Marston up for focused on auditory processing: **the Method New York Autism**

Vestibular Auditory Integration Spectrum Center, founded by Valerie Dejean. We invested in this from 2003–2010.

In 2006, we discovered **Play Attention**, the world's number one neurocognitive program for training executive functions (mental control and self-regulation). Play Attention was invented by Dr. David Belkm. A biofeedback system is used for training kids with ADHD. We enrolled Marston in Dr. Belkm's two hours/day, three days/week program. We stayed in this program until 2016.

In 2008, we reenrolled Marston in the **Sensory Learning Center** in Boulder, Colorado to help with any residual sensory integration problems that weren't fully resolved during his time with IAHP. We stuck with this program until 2015.

Dr. Harry Wachs was another renowned figure my warrior moms and I had our eyes on. He was a pioneer in the field of developmental optometry, and he'd expanded his practice to studying the vision problems of children with brain developmental disorders and disabilities.

Dr. Wachs was an optometrist by training but found vision—how the mind comprehends the things it sees—more fascinating than the process of sight itself. He obtained a degree in optometry in the forties. By the fifties, he'd opened a contact lens store, one of the first of its kind. Shortly thereafter, he teamed up with psychologist Arnold Gesell and embarked on a lifelong career of studying vision, movement, and child development. This fascination with advancing cognitive development via visual methods led to another professional association with Jean Piaget and Hans Furth. Wachs and Furth brought Piaget's groundbreaking educational theories to the United Sates, and they eventually established a school for thinking in West Virginia. This experience was delineated in the book *Thinking Goes to School*. Wachs and Furth became professors at Catholic University in Washington, DC. Wachs eventually ended up at George Washington University, in the School of Education's Reading Center, where, in the early 1980s, he started the Visual & Conceptual Development Center, specializing in helping children with autism and other developmental disabilities.

He worked with everyone from Saudi Arabian princes to underprivileged children. There was a special program for professional athletes, particularly quarterbacks, who wanted to improve their game through hand-eye coordination linked to understanding their visual field. Imagine what a quarterback can achieve if they can cut the time it takes to assess the defense—from the snap to the pass—in half. Wachs made this possible with his revolutionary **Vision Therapy**, and the Redskins can attest to it, as his method was incorporated into their QB training program. He co-authored his second and final book with Serena Wieder, PhD,

Visual/Spatial Portals to Thinking, Feeling and Movement, which is a culmination of his work with children on the autism spectrum.

Dr. Harry Wachs was in DC keynoting a conference in the early 2000s. *I'm attending this whether it's for doctors or medical professionals or whomever. I am going.*

We were able to meet with Dr. Wachs afterward. In a matter of minutes, he assessed Marston and suggested a treatment plan. Of course, I couldn't travel to and from DC weekly to go to his learning center; I needed someone to come to me.

I hired my godson William's sister, Crystal, to accompany me to Washington, DC. Crystal was an exceptionally bright college student who was interested in the medical field. She was a quick learner under the tutelage of Dr. Wachs. She and I both learned the concepts, protocols, and how to implement them to help Marston progress. Marston was home schooled, so she would come to our house daily to help me execute the Wachs program.

Shortly thereafter, Dr. Harry Wachs created a visual concept computer program called the *Lexia Program*, which we were able to use remotely for five years until 2009. His program was dubbed "comprehensive intervention," as it was that intense.

The process of improving cognitive ability starts simply with memorization exercises. Marston would do something like put a red, green, and blue block on a white piece of paper, and then he'd study the arrangement for thirty seconds. Then, Crystal would undo the design, hide the blocks for a minute, and then give them back, asking him to recreate the original pattern. This improves visual memory. Because Marston had a hard time with memory in general, we saw improvements fast. And, even more exciting, we discovered Marston was a visual learner. This was a big deal. Now, we knew that to teach Marston successfully, we needed to show him how to do something versus tell him.

You can use Vision Therapy to improve visual perception and visual processing for just about anything—from improving memory to strengthening a lazy eye to improving defensive driving abilities to stopping migraines in people with eye-tracking issues. Visual Therapy can improve overall focus, help a musician read music more effectively, increase visual acuity—the list goes on. I met a young woman that couldn't pass the bar exam; she underwent Visual Therapy and eventually passed.

Marston worked with a Visual Therapist for eight years total, until he was thirteen, improving his cognitive abilities and changing the course of his life dramatically.

We discussed diet regularly and read articles on proper nutrition and its benefits regarding various diseases and disorders, including autism, and its role in inflammation. We have monitored Marston's nutritional intake since birth and continue to assist and direct him to this day. Medical doctors throughout the years have helped us with our biomedical/nutritional treatment plan.

•°•°•°•

Being overwhelmed by life due to a sick child is not relegated to any category of people like rich or poor, American or foreign, black or white. Stress does not discriminate, but it can inhibit people from seeking answers. It can stifle forward motion. This is why we need to keep talking about it and helping each other. This is why we need to unite; we warrior moms need to stick together.

We collected data like any good research group. Then, we'd evaluate our findings and implement new therapies or medications when we felt confident enough. Sometimes, we'd see immediate results that fizzled fast; sometimes, a new therapy elicited subtler results over time. And, sometimes, we didn't see any change. On realizing we were gaining momentum but still having not found a cure, we'd move on to the next new discovery on brain injury or autism.

We are still networking, collecting information, sharing our successes and failures, and supporting each other to this day. Warrior moms we will always be.

9

"THIS IS JUST LIFE...."

"The weak can never forgive. Forgiveness is an attribute of
the strong."

—Mahatma Gandhi

WITH MARSTON IN SCHOOL FULL-TIME, it allowed me the
opportunity to start volunteering at Austin's school and work part-
time for Eric (on a steadier basis), helping him open his new
practice.

Austin was in middle school by this point, so they didn't need
me inside his classroom cutting out shapes or gluing felt onto
construction paper. I'd work in the lunchroom or peddle the cart
around that had pencils and erasers and books for sale, going from
class to class. I chaperoned all of Austin's school trips to museums
and the planetarium, to special sporting events, or to an outing at

the park or the movies. Even the middle school dances—I chaperoned those, too.

Austin never complained about anything. He was glad to see me, or so it seemed. Although, he didn't need me or need anything by that point. The space between us was apparent. It had been five, six, seven years that I'd devoted to Marston.

This was one of the toughest truths for me to accept—that in trying to break down Marston's wall, one had been erected between Austin and me. I hadn't been the one to build it, per se; circumstance did that—autism did it—but that mattered little in the grand scheme.

A few years back, Austin started a software company with some buddies. It was out in Arizona. They did well with their launch and turned around and sold it in no time. I was able to fly there to see him during that time. It gave me an opportunity to be alone with my oldest child and to apologize, finally, for my reaction to the unforeseen circumstances of our lives, for my unstoppable drive to help Marston. Austin said it was okay. He reminded me there was nothing to apologize for. It was what it was.

Why do I feel so bad?

Why does my heart ache still?

I remember looking up at the sky when Austin was a toddler, the easiest of kids, and thinking, *Is this parenting, God? What a breeze....* Honestly, it was laughable. Maybe I looked up one too many times.

Maybe I was asking for a dare with all my cutesy smiles and confidence. Maybe, one day, God had finally had enough: "I hear you, Chris. You think parenting is a breeze? Hold on for this wild ride!"

I never expected my mother to tell me she was sorry for caring so diligently for Paula, and she never did. I've never looked back on my life (as her child) with resentment, even though Margaret mentioned how she'd always wished I had known the mom that raised her.

Austin, my first child, my perfect boy, my brainiac, my athlete, my entrepreneur, my kind son who has stood quietly on the sidelines of our journey with his brother, my son who practices transcendental meditation and yoga, who has become the man who asks nothing of his parents—that man has finally helped me to understand that *this is just life*....

People live decades before they become cognizant that we are here to practice our humanness toward others. This is the point. Austin learned that within his first six years of life. I'd watch him play baseball in the park with his friends for fun, bringing Marston along just so he could be near other kids. Austin was usually the team captain in these games. I'd watch him always pick the smallest kid first, or the slowest—the one who would normally get picked last in gym class. He knew God had given him the goods when it came to sports. We all knew. And he never took advantage of that. He used this gift to include everyone, to be the kind of athlete and leader people gravitate toward—one with compassion, confidence, drive, and gratitude. He used his powers for good, so to speak.

Austin attempted to play baseball in college at the University of Arizona, but he tore the labrum in his right shoulder during tryouts, and it changed all that. He said he wanted to rush a fraternity, anyway, and, having received an academic scholarship and being in the honors college, the injury was a blessing in disguise. He wouldn't have been able to do it all, at least not to his perfectionistic standards.

He currently lives in Southern California, in a section of West L.A. that he refers to as Brentwood adjacent (or maybe West Hollywood adjacent). I visit, and I swear you could jump off Interstate 405 onto his balcony. He is that close to the freeway! But, he and his roommate don't complain. They say they love it, then point to a nearby high school football field and say they crack beers and watch games for free during the season. To them, it's a real treat.

He doesn't talk to me about his romantic life. I get too wrapped up in it, and he doesn't want me to worry. I think I got depressed after a couple breakups, and that was more than he could take. My brain, my emotions, my time are generally booked to capacity. Austin knows that and has never wanted to add to it. I guess that might be part of it, too.

It's not your fault, Mom, it's just life....

I know I'm supposed to believe that. But, Austin doesn't have siblings like I do to bounce all this off of, so it's not the same. He doesn't even have a traditional brotherly relationship with Marston. He's been a father figure since the age of six. He has Will, who's like a brother, so I do find comfort in that. And, he knows how much we love him. Of course he knows.

I guess it's neither my place nor in my power to fix everything.

There might be a lesson in here for me, too.

•°•°•°•

Eric's new practice is forty minutes away. (I wonder how many times I've listened to *Barney* on the way there and back and never caught myself.) Twenty years ago, opening a private practice was still prevalent—not like today, where belonging to a group is the trend. Eric, needing to focus on the surgery end of things, needed someone he could rely on to do the books. A lot can go amiss when you're in practice alone. To this day, I go into the office whenever I want (one of the perks of sleeping with the boss) as part of the accounting team. Life at home was so busy, with the bustle of helpers going in and out, and some form of therapy—or two or three—being implemented 'round the clock, it was nice to see Eric at work on a regular basis. It was calming.

Due to my desire to be on "makeup duty" (making up for all the time that had been taken away from Eric and Austin), my schedule wasn't any lighter with Marston being in school full-time. But, it did feel different and more diversified. I was able to spend more time with adults, more time with myself doing research or traveling to conferences. I think the change helped me recover physically from the rigor of the IAHP programs, and from life in fifth gear in general.

10

THE POWER OF WORDS

"You have been assigned this mountain to show others it can be moved."

—Translated from the Book of Matthew

2003–2007

IN OUR SECOND YEAR AT Montessori Discovery, when Marston was seven, the principle retired. The new principal had no children of her own, which I've used as an excuse time and again to justify her behavior. The truth is that it's probably narrow minded of me to assume a person without kids couldn't have compassion for us and for Marston. I guess she was probably not the kind of person who went the extra mile to help kids in need, and it was as simple as that. She kicked Marston out of the program, stating he didn't have the "skills" to keep up with his classmates, and it was affecting the esteem and attitudes of the so-called normal kids. I am certain Maria Montessori rolled over in her grave that day. Her whole teaching method was founded on her early work with kids that were different from the so-called normal ones.

This was devastating.

Fortunately, the Weiss family wasn't comprised of people that sit still for too long. We were confident we'd find Marston a new fit before long. No sooner did we take a few deep breaths and dry our eyes than we started working toward that goal.

•°•°•°•

The power of my father's words kept my chin up during the first seven years of Marston's life as much as the progress that had finally happened thanks to the program at the IAHP. Then, there were my warrior moms: they picked up where Dad and The Institutes left off. This collection of forces fueled my drive and my soul. But, keep in mind, there was still nothing out there. There was no talk of a spectrum despite the buzz about other things. So, I was (*we were*) running full-speed ahead, but no one knew where we were running to; there was certainly no finish line in sight.

In 1997, the reauthorization of the federal special education law, which has since been renamed the Individuals with Disabilities Education Act (IDEA), was reaffirmed. This law, revamped from the Regular Education Initiative of the mid-eighties, required that children with disabilities be educated "to the maximum extent possible" in the "least restrictive environment" possible. Up to this point, children with disabilities that were considered mild in nature could be part of a regular classroom environment, but a child with a severe handicap, like say the inability to speak, was educated predominantly in a closed-off setting with other severely impaired children.

To what extent is inclusion healthy for a brain-injured child and the so-called normal children around him? That topic is being argued to this day. I'm a firm believer that inclusion generally teaches not only compassion but the importance of community to regular kids. And, I believe it helps special needs kids develop social skills, emotional intelligence, book skills—the skills of life!

Unlike when Marston was in elementary school, autism has become common as we embark on the third decade in the new millennium. Inclusion has become the standard. Having a hired aide, a paraprofessional for the special needs child, is also the norm. But, we certainly don't have this method mastered. Most paraprofessionals aren't even trained to handle special needs kids. Most teachers still aren't. And the assessment process is tedious and subjective. Just as knowledge of autism and treatment of the disorder is in its infancy, so, too, is the management and education of individuals diagnosed with the disorder.

Imagine what it was like for us and all the other families trying to help their brain-injured children back then....

The law was updated and passed when Marston was just two years old (1997), giving him the right to be in a normal classroom;

yet, in the 2003–2004 school year, when he was seven, he was thrown out for being just that—a special needs student in a classroom full of regular kids. We had no recourse. Moving forward, we didn't know where to turn. Legally, we were not sure if we had options, but it was a private school. Those come with their own rules. Time was against us, and money was a factor. Eric had been working overtime (and at two jobs) since Marston was born to keep up with all the therapies we were trying. We didn't have extra money left over to fight the system on top of everything else; all our money went to living expenses and to Marston.

Our local doctors continued to say things like "give him time" and "boys develop more slowly than girls." With all I was doing, I was still being treated like an idiot, even though I had Austin (a pretty decent marker as to how a normal boy develops) and now a string of professional markers, too (the Developmental Profiles from The Institutes), documenting Marston's initial capabilities and gauging his progress from there.

Even after stats on autism and its unprecedented rise in babies was evidenced, there was still rampant ignorance of the disorder among the medical community. And, the media only made matters worse. Nonetheless, with the most progressive school around booting us out—a school that was dedicated to the individual child and to different styles of learning—we were in search of a place that didn't seem to exist.

The mission to find a place that would accept Marston led us to the University of North Florida and, specifically, to their Department of Special Education. The chairperson was Karen Patterson, PhD. We described our dilemma to her, along with our needs and desires. She felt homeschooling with a quality teacher, while attempting to find the right classroom setting, was the best chance we had at obtaining our goals. At least homeschooling could start sooner rather than later while we worked on everything else— everyone agreed on that. I asked for her best student. She gave us the name Karin Hunt without hesitation. (As an aside, I believe God puts people in your life for a reason; Karin was God-sent.)

Karin was an older student, late thirties, graduating with a 4.0 in special education. She was married to a military man. They had two children, a son Marston's age and an older daughter. She would change our lives as well as Marston's.

Next, we found a suitable classroom environment for him. It was a small school with a wonderful administrator, Jim Schultz. He was a professional educator with undergraduate and master's degrees from Kent State. He embraced both Marston and Karin. So, from 2003–2004, Marston was enrolled in **Center Academy**.

Center Academy had small class sizes, individualized lesson plans, and adjustable curriculum so that it was developmentally appropriate.

This worked well enough to get us through the next year.

But, it was obvious we needed more help. A truly unique and individualized education plan for Marston was destined to be the only route. I was happy he was able to be in a classroom environment for another year. No progress had been made with special needs kids and inclusion in that timeframe or with individualized lesson plans. But, one thing had been accomplished on our end: Marston was comfortable in a group setting, even if he couldn't participate. (You probably noticed we were hiring *and paying* our own in-class tutors. That's how far we've come in the last decade.)

It wasn't that Marston wasn't making any progress; it just appeared to be negligible when compared to that of the other kids. Being his mom, I could see him taking it all in, but with his speech issues, it really didn't seem obvious to most other people, including his educators.

After watching from the sidelines for that school year, Karin felt the need to take over, anyway. We had full confidence in her vision for Marston by that point, so we let her.

She transformed a spare bedroom at her house into a classroom.

Marston started attending Karin's school in lieu of any schools with traditional classroom settings. (He would end up attending her school until he was eighteen years old.) She brought Marston in as one of her own, and she coordinated his therapy around his schoolwork.

We worked together to devise an educational plan, as well as a curriculum that would be the most beneficial to him moving forward, with the goal being to prepare him to live successfully and on his own (as much as possible) in the real world. Benefits would include not only book learning, but social skills and life skills such as cooking, cleaning, hygiene, dressing, grooming, etc.

Our plan was intensive, and we were excited about it. (Keep in mind, we still didn't know how to get Marston to read effectively or how teach him how to retain that type of information.) Our efforts in developing this personalized educational plan to the best of our abilities led us to discover an emeritus professor at Columbia's School of Education, **Marion Blank, PhD**.

Dr. Blank's ability to teach, understand an individual's issues and needs, and diagnose problems seemed unmatched in the education of special needs students (*and regular students*) at the time, at least according to our research (mine, Karin's, and my warrior moms' group).

Dr. Blank had made a name for herself as a revolutionary teacher. She was the creator of the Light on Literacy and Reading Kingdom programs, where she's authored over three dozen workbooks teaching the skills of reading.

Other works, like *The Reading Remedy*, *Spectacular Bond*, and *ASD Typing* (her later works), are devoted to teaching children with ASD how to read.

The inability to read effectively impacts more than 33 percent of children in our school systems nationwide. Blank has devoted her life to obliterating this issue. She is the recipient of the Upton Sinclair Award for her significant and courageous contribution to education, as well as a winner of the Special Education Software Award, and her list of achievements goes on and on. In her eighties at the time of this writing, Dr. Blank is still authoring books that teach parents and children alike how to achieve their intended intellectual potential.

I gave Eric her name, and he tracked her down. Finally, arriving at a phone number, he called.

"I'm retired. I'm too old."

All of her responses, which were plentiful, fell on deaf ears. My husband told her she had one more life to change.

In a couple of days, we were sitting in her living room just outside New York City.

She worked with Marston for no more than three or four minutes and said, "This will be easy. I can teach anybody to read." Dr. Marion Blank was a tough lady and demanded excellence and a steadfast dedication to her methods. She didn't care what we had tried, and she certainly didn't care what his "current teacher," Karin, had learned in the past. In fact, she thought most of what teachers had been taught about education was garbage. She was a visionary.

For this reason, Karin, as much as Marston, became a pupil of her method.

She devised Marston's academic plan, which was focused on reading, as well as a socialization schedule, and she created concrete benchmarks to reach goals in the other area where he was most weak: speech. But, and I want to stress this, reading was paramount.

Karin was amazing. She had rearranged her life and home to devote her new career as an educator to the one and only Marston. And, now, we were asking her to let go of years of schooling and her own natural instincts for Dr. Blank's method. Thankfully, Karin saw Dr. Blank's genius from the start, swallowed some pride, and worked with her tirelessly. She implemented Blank's "get Marston to read" plan and called her regularly with updates and to seek ongoing advice. (I want to note that Karin was not our first choice for learning Dr. Blank's method. We'd initially thought it best to hire a second tutor while Karin focused on life skills. We were wrong. The first educator didn't make the cut. Dr. Blank put a quick stop to it with a "don't waste my time" declaration. *Okay….*)

Marston and I took quarterly trips to New York to meet with Dr. Blank on weekends.

Marston did not take to Dr. Blank easily. She was militant in her training of him; whereas, most people treated him like a person with special needs: slow to discipline, quick to praise. I think she scared him most of the time. He'd stare at her wide-eyed when she talked. It was almost comical how his eyes were all "woo!" as if they'd lost the ability to blink. Dr. Blank didn't have time for praise. Her environment was one of learning. No nonsense. Period. After her initial training, we would fly there periodically, too, when we needed tune-ups. Doctor Blank also came down to Ponte Vedra Beach.

I was never trained enough, like Karin had been, to teach her method, and I hesitate to simplify it, but what Dr. Blank recognized in a matter of minutes on the day she first met Marston was that his mind understood individual letters but couldn't comprehend what would happen to them when they were put together. This meant that Marston, and kids whose minds worked like his, needed to learn each letter in the alphabet and then learn letter combinations such as th, st, ph, ing, ed, str, ch, sh, sch, ee, ae, ai, ei, ie, ing, tion, ly, etc., because they are an extension of the alphabet, if you will. (Again, this is just scratching the surface.) She drew a series of lines in patterns on a chalkboard during that first meeting, too, stating everything is about patterns, understanding them and memorizing them. It looked like Roman numerals or chicken scratch to me. It took Eric about two seconds before he announced, "That's elephant." He was right.

I remember sitting in the auditorium during Eric's graduation ceremony from Davidson. As I looked over the list of students, I felt terrible they'd forgotten his name. And then I found it under magna cum laude. Needless to say, Marion and Eric would bond bigtime during the years we worked with her, discussing everything under the sun from Marston to physics, religion, politics, movies, and the weather.

Marston had been able to follow simple instructions to a T for some time. In addition to his gait being corrected so that he didn't slouch and now looked normal when he walked, his mood and emotions were being conveyed accurately through facial expressions. I was able to determine what he was understanding and what he wasn't from the look on his face or from him telling me in a word or two. This is the comprehension I've been talking about. But, he could not put sentences together beyond three or four words tops, and when he did speak those simple sentences, he sounded young, like a toddler. And, he couldn't read at all. Even though he could recognize and remember shapes and sometimes the shape of a word, he had no understanding of it.

After two years with Karin implementing Dr. Blank's methodology, Marston was able to read at the fifth-grade level—a stunning accomplishment. As his literacy skills improved, so did his ability to communicate verbally. Dr. Blank's program was (and has always been) about improving reading and writing skills. She has always argued that too much emphasis is being put on the spoken word in lieu of mastering the art of reading and writing, which, by the way, is the number one skill necessary to achieve your max potential. How are kids who are nonverbal going to communicate if they are not taught the skills of reading and writing?

In addition to her initial method of teaching kids letter patterns and combinations, Dr. Marion Blank's method uses an "intensive word teaching" system where every component of a word is taught in a comprehensive and integrated manner. After a student understands the individual letters, they learn letter combinations, then spelling, then a word's meaning, its relationship to other words, its placement in sentences, etc. It's all broken down. These processes are applied to even the small, seemingly meaningless words like *some, but, and, or, that, if, of, our, his, the,* etc. Those words, which are often so weak in children with ASD (like Marston), are critical to effective language use. Mastering their use transforms language skills.

Reading is commonly dissected into two major areas: **decoding,** or figuring out the words by what the letters "say," and **comprehension**, or understanding the message that the words are saying.

I feel like, until recently, it hasn't occurred to doctors and educators that nonverbal children on the spectrum can learn to communicate through the written word. An inability to speak does not mean an inability to understand or learn. Like I'd been saying about Marston since he'd started IAHP, his awareness was skyrocketing. He was beginning to understand everything.

There are books on the market today written by nonverbal adults on the spectrum like *Ido in Autismland* and *Carly's Voice: Breaking through Autism,* to name a couple. Check them out when you get a chance. You wouldn't believe how much a person who doesn't speak actually has to say.

Facilitative communication, developed at Syracuse University, has done wonders in our autistic community.

Typing to communicate or Facilitated Communication (FC) is a form of Alternative and Augmentative Communication (AAC) in which people with disabilities and communication impairments express themselves by pointing (e.g., at pictures, letters, or objects) and, more commonly, by typing (e.g., with a keyboard).

They make great use of iPads using this technique. People who couldn't communicate regularly—well, their lives have been changed thanks to these kinds of breakthroughs in communication.

Of course, I had been talking to everyone and researching like a madwoman since Marston's birth, and, still, Dr. Marion Blank's method and others that fall under this classification were mostly new to me. There was still so much to learn.

It makes perfect sense that reading, writing, and comprehending material effectively should be the number one goal in the education of our children, even though the emphasis has never seemed to be on that over speaking. Think about it: every school has a speech therapist. Parents flip out when their child gets to a certain age and can't pronounce words as clearly as their peers do. These children are being pulled from classrooms, where they are learning reading and reading comprehension, so that they might learn to speak more effectively.

Dr. Marion Blank's parents did not know how to write when they arrived in America. They literally signed an X for their names as they went through Ellis Island. She went on, as a woman in the 1950s and a first-generation American, to receive degrees from City College in NYC and Columbia University and to be one of the first women to receive her PhD from Cambridge.

Dr. Blank's educational guidance was instrumental in making Marston who he is today. Her methods were profound and life changing. We thank God everyday she saw it in her heart to take on one more student.

11

YOU'VE GOT TO HAVE FAITH

"God never made a promise that was too good to be true."

—Dwight L. Moody

2008, 2009

MARSTON WAS AT THE AGE where Catholic kids received their confirmation. He wasn't going to a regular school because he was with Karin, but we'd always had him enrolled in church activities and signed up for the classes that went along with receiving all the sacraments since his baptism.

Thanks to all the work of IAHP and Karin and Dr. Blank's methodology, Marston had been reading for a couple years now and was speaking better. He was not capable of retaining information to the point of being able to recite it, though. He could memorize pieces of songs and poems and prayers, but nothing in its entirety.

Part of the ceremony of confirmation entails each teen recite a series of standard Catholic prayers such as the Lord's Prayer, Hail Mary, Glory Be, the Apostles' Creed, the Ten Commandments.... You have to be "ready" to be confirmed and seen as an adult by the church in order to take the sacrament. Even though we were putting in all the hours necessary at CCD, Marston couldn't memorize these prayers. He did a decent job of getting through them when prompted—when the CCD teacher or I assisted with lead-ins to each line. But, it didn't matter how much we practiced, he simply couldn't retain this kind of written information.

Well, about two weeks before his CCD class was being confirmed, the director of the program informed me that Marston wasn't going to be able to participate in the ceremony.

We were blindsided by the news. We'd figured everyone knew Marston's brain didn't work like the other kids' brains going into this. We thought everything was fine. Plus, the church—being a place of unconditional love and forgiveness, a place where kindness and nonjudgment are foundational—would make an exception to the "rules" of confirmation for Marston. Eric and I didn't discuss this as a possible outcome of all these months of classes or all our hard work. We both just assumed.... I had viewed confirmation like I'd viewed the Montessori schools and swim lessons: Marston and I did what we always do. I was on the move, trying everything I could to educate him while immersing him into the real world like we did with Austin, like any parents do with their child, and

Marston, bless his heart, was going along with all of it. Confirmation, sacrament or not, was no exception to this rule. We tossed him into the classes, and he worked his tail off to be a successful student and learn the prayers.

My heart broke when they called with the news that he couldn't be confirmed. Well, I think I was more in shock—since I was one of the volunteer teachers in the CCD class—but my heart was on the verge of breaking.

When I told Eric, he reacted a little differently. He was angry and made several phone calls over as many days to the church to remedy the situation. We were never called back. By that point, we were both so emotional, I was ready to deliver a handwritten plea to the pope himself, asking the Church to reconsider.

A few days passed while Eric and I tried to land on a plan that was somewhere between me flying to Rome and marching into the Vatican, and him calling our church again. We ended up going with Eric's plan. For the fifth time, Eric got the machine. After that, we went upstairs to regroup. I wiped away a tear that had strayed in the heat of my frustration as I marched up the stairs, and I remember saying, "Gimmie a frigging break, Marston's going to be the first person in heaven! C'mon!"

Then, Eric and I sat on the bed, calmed down, and said a prayer.

During this prayer, the phone rang.

The Caller ID said Saint Edwards Church, a church we had never heard of.

On seeing that, I blurted: "Don't answer it. They probably want money, and they're on my shit list right now."

Eric gave me the "calm down, Chris" look and put the call on speaker. "Hello?"

"Hi there," the man on the other end said. "You probably don't remember me. I'm Father Cowart. I baptized Marston sixteen years ago."

I started crying outright.

Father Cowart went on to tell us he'd been traveling and working all over Europe and hadn't come back to the States until recently. He was the parish priest at Saint Edwards in Starke, Florida, a prison ministry, just two hours west of us.

He'd been going through belongings and reorganizing when he came upon a box of letters he'd saved throughout his travels. This was where he found my *thank you* note and the picture of him baptizing Marston. This was his first sacrament as a priest. It was a special memory imprinted on his heart. Then, he said, "As I held your correspondence in my hand, it spoke to me, so I had to call. How is everyone?"

Father Cowart didn't know Marston was autistic. He didn't know anything about our lives. We'd only met each other once! For the next hour on the phone with Father Cowart, I threw up: I verbally regurgitated the string of events from the baptism back in '95 to Marston being denied confirmation five days ago.

He told us not to worry, that he'd confirm our son, no problem.

A week later, we drove to Starke. This tiny town is very Baptist, with a population of around five thousand and a prison as the main attraction. The church was a small, wooden structure, with twenty-four pews, and the social building was a trailer. A far cry from the grandiose church in Ponte Vedra.

It was amazing to see Father Cowart after all those years. He did not have good news for us, however. He needed Marston's parish to release his papers to St. Edwards Church (*his church*) so Marston could be confirmed there. Our church denied Father Cowart. Because of Marston's special needs, they did not believe Marston could participate in church life as they deemed appropriate and acceptable.

Father Cowart told us to be patient. He promised the answer would reveal itself. As you can imagine from reading to this point, it became my mission to educate and integrate Marston into the world, which included being confirmed, and patience wasn't exactly one of my top virtues. But, I heeded the advice of Father Cowart and put on the brakes.

We started attending Saint Edwards once or twice a month. It was such a warm and welcoming environment. This routine went on for eight or nine months. During this time, a new archbishop from Cuba took over in the St. Augustine district. Father Cowart said it was time to go to the man with the power. Without hesitation, the new archbishop gave Marston special dispensation to get confirmed by Father Cowart.

For anybody who's not familiar with a Catholic confirmation, it usually takes place during a mass with teens at the altar getting confirmed collectively. Afterward, the families often all go their separate ways to celebrate how they see fit, like at the end of any given mass.

I've always believed that when something bad happens, if you believe strongly enough and keep the faith, you will be rewarded for your endurance. I witnessed this firsthand on the day of Marston's confirmation.

That day, at Saint Edwards Church, he was the only person being confirmed. He sat at the altar with Father Cowart, and the whole ceremony was for him. It was standing room only. Father Cowart talked about Marston, incorporating his story and his courage into the mass, highlighting his life and achievements, particularly during the sermon.

After the ceremony, as if I weren't already overwhelmed enough, they asked us to stay, as the church family had prepared a luncheon in Marston's honor. The spread was like nothing I'd ever seen—all set up in that small, unassuming mobile building next to the church. The joy that we felt that day…well, I cried all through his ceremony and all through lunch. I probably looked nuts after a while, but everyone just kept hugging me and Eric and Marston, and it was bliss. Austin was in college in Arizona, so he couldn't attend, but he would have loved it. The event was beyond my wildest dreams, watching Marston be celebrated like that.

It's not the ordinary building that makes the church; it's the extraordinary people in the building that make the church. Father Cowart had been telling Marston's story for weeks and months prior to the confirmation. His whole parish had been praying for Marston to be able to be confirmed in their church. The lunch afterward was extravagant, like a wedding reception but with Marston being the honoree. It was amazing. When God makes things happen, he does it on a grand scale. We have always believed that when one door closes, a bigger one opens.

Some of these stories are tricky to tell, as the point isn't to place blame or judgment or to direct focus to the obstacles that have placed themselves in our path time and again. As I have spent my life trying to help my son, it's time for me to help other parents with kids (and adult children) with ASD. And, the only way I can do that effectively is by speaking our truth.

This disorder is isolating. Our stories make us stronger and create commonality. They bring us together, soothe us, blanket our weary souls, and remind us to have faith. Many of our stories have turned out to be pieces in the autism puzzle. This is the purpose of this memoir.

When I think of our journey and the collection of stories that comprise *Educating Marston*, I don't dwell on the pain and the obstacles. I remember the victories that have brought us one step closer to Marston living a life of purpose with as much normalcy as possible. When I think of this story specifically, I remember the miracle of Father Cowart's phone call that dark afternoon. I remember the kindness, patience, and tenacity he demonstrated for nearly a year afterward. I recall the dispensation that was granted by the archbishop. He had compassion, and he believed in Marston's story even though he had never met him. And, I remember the open arms of a parish that was tucked inside a small town in a Baptist community that was over two hours away.

12

WHAT COMES AFTER "HI"?

"The point is that everyone needs exposure to the various ways of life...."

—Arthur Alexander

2009–2013

WE SO-CALLED NORMAL FOLKS HAVE probably underestimated the significance of being able to do certain givens in a typical, middle-class, American life. Here are some generalized givens: It's a given that when we grow up, we'll get a job. It's a given we'll have a bank account (or two), a home (whether we rent or own), and, with it, bills to pay. It's a given we'll learn how to pay those bills. It's a given we'll bathe regularly, buy groceries, go the movies, prepare a meal. We'll own a phone and call up friends and family to chat. The majority of us will drive and even own a car. And, we'll drive that car through a drive-thru at some point and order coffee or food. I imagine the vast majority of adults have ordered from a drive-thru at least once in their lives.

What if these things were not givens?

What if you didn't naturally understand how to talk on the phone or pay for groceries or order a cup of coffee from a drive-thru, even though you were raised in an environment where people did these sorts of things every day? What then?

Like I've said about the progress with Marston, I knew information was finally going in—I could see it on his face—but it still wasn't coming out. After learning to read, it was Karin's primary job to teach him how to interact with the world around him and improve upon his executive functions.

The term *executive functions* refers to the hypothesized brain processes that control other brain processes. Metaphorically speaking, the executive functions can collectively be described as the brain's chief executive officer. Executive functions include, at a minimum, inhibition, memory, attention, flexibility, planning, and problem solving—activities that are critical to everyday functioning in life. People who have difficulty inhibiting themselves, remembering things, planning, problem solving, and/or being flexible in their thinking will present with major deficiencies in social, academic, and vocational functioning. Unfortunately, children with autism spectrum disorder

(ASD) commonly suffer from deficits in many or all of these areas, yet there is very little agreement or clarity across the various disciplines involved in autism treatment regarding what executive functions actually are and how, if at all, they can be improved.

While Marston wasn't the kind of kid who needed help controlling himself or his moods, socially, he was at an extreme disadvantage compared to other kids. He knew he was different. He was intimidated by that. His brain didn't work logically. Never mind that his speech was limited, but even when he talked to me—and I understood him—his mind didn't work in an A-B-C fashion. He'd tell a story and start in the middle, then jump to the end, then back to the beginning. He was aware of this. This was one of the reasons he preferred to remain quiet in group settings, why he never bothered the other kids. Because his brain didn't go to the logical way of doing things first, he had to be taught everything. And, by everything, I mean we had to teach Marston how to perform everyday tasks that are accomplished involuntarily by the time most of us reach adulthood. It was up to his below-average memory to kick into high gear and retain the skills the rest of us take for granted, many of which fall under the category of executive functions.

Karin would make him watch movies. (The method she used was taught to her by Marion Blank.) *Born Free* is one of the movies that comes to mind. She'd stop it every five or ten minutes, and they'd discuss what they'd viewed.

"Marston, what just happened?"

"Lion got killed."

"What will happen to the lion's babies now?"

"Orphans."

Then, Karin would make him retell the last ten minutes of the movie, scene by scene. Given that movies are considered 80 percent visual, a lot of scenes can fit into a ten-minute span in a movie. These kinds of exercises worked to strengthen his visual memory, his expressive skills (retelling the events of the movie), and his cognitive abilities (remembering and retaining the information).

She'd say to me (another Marion Blank directive), "Chris, when you go home this evening, have Marston watch you cook dinner and make sure to narrate yourself as you go. Say every step out loud and ask him to repeat it. If you have a recipe—say, you're making chocolate chip cookies—make him read the instructions out loud." She suggested that breaking down even simple tasks into steps, like a list, would help. People love lists—and numbering helps. Think about it: if you forget your grocery list but remembered you had fifteen items on it, you'll likely come up with all the items as you shop. I had already been doing things like this since his birth. We'd see a fire truck, and I'd explain what it did, what color it was. I'd point out the hose and the firemen. I'd talk about the station from which the truck came. I'd explain what fire was and how fires started. Karin reminded me to keep it up.

She taught Marston how to raise his hand when he had a question. He was afraid to be called on, afraid to have other kids hear him fumble through a question. He didn't like ordering in public for that reason. We'd have to constantly say, "Speak up, honey, we can't hear you." He'd do it. He'd repeat himself and speak up; however, he was very uncomfortable. Talking to strangers and ordering for yourself can be stressful for lots of kids, and even some adults. I've seen plenty of children lack the skills and confidence for ordering their own meal, whispering into a parent's ear, having difficulty making eye contact; these are abilities that come with practice. In Marston's case, he needed lots of practice. He still has difficulty reading a menu today. Most menus have rows and columns and pictures. They don't have the kind of order a book does, making them more challenging for someone with a brain injury to comprehend.

"How do I talk to people?" Marston asked Karin one day.

Ordering a meal is one thing. The server is right at the table asking, "What can I get you to eat?" What about general greetings and chitchat? Marston didn't understand how to strike up a conversation with a classmate or a kid at the park or one sitting next him at one of Austin's baseball games.

What comes after "hi"?

This question goes through the minds of kids with autism. We take things like this for granted. And we forget that everyone has feelings. No matter how smart or average a person appears to be, our emotions are on a more level playing field (generally speaking). Everyone experiences happiness and sorrow, anger, joy, fear, surprise. We get lonely; this is part of life. Kids on the spectrum feel just as deeply as the rest of us, but they often sound different. They have more issues with confidence compared to regular kids, and they don't know what comes after "hi." In addition, they don't want attention directed toward them. Nerves only make their ability to focus and succeed in social situations worse.

Karin would say, "Pretend I'm a girl in your math class, Marston. You're sitting next to me. Let's start talking."

She started roleplaying like this regularly. It was the only way to get him out of his shell. Karin ultimately started an acting class with Marston. It was improv and mimicked real-life situations.

With Dr. Blank's method and Karin's life skills classes, Marston was gaining on the game of life. But, he was back in a classroom of one, much like his life as a toddler. We wanted more for him. Why not put some of these skills to the test in the real world?

One of her ideas was to get Marston into a real class at one of the local high schools. We found one that let him enroll in an ROTC class and an art class. They were elective courses. Then, we jumped on the extracurricular activity bandwagon, because a kid needs to play, too.

We didn't know what he would or could retain. We were basically throwing everything we could think of at him, hoping some of it would stick.

He took swimming lessons.

We signed him up for horseback riding. What we actually signed him up for was called hypotherapy. This type of treatment is a:

Therapeutic method in which the horse is used for the rehabilitation, integration, and physical, psychological, emotional and social development of the person. It is a rehabilitating activity and recognized all over the world. The benefits are a general feeling of well-being.

Dog companion therapy is really popular nowadays. I looked for the perfect dog for Marston. I eventually chose a Coton de Tulear: a small, white dog known for its ability to bond with an individual and help with anxiety. Tinkerbell truly (but not classically trained) became a service dog. People are using dogs for all sorts of issues beyond the traditional seeing-eye dog, a service that started with four certified dogs in the UK in the 1930s. A company in South Carolina uses service dogs to help kids (and adults) with ASD improve their socialization skills.

We started playing audiobooks at bedtime. Osmosis? Maybe? Who knows, but we figured, it couldn't hurt!

Taekwondo: He studied this martial art until he reached black belt level. In Taekwondo, the stances (or positions) build on one another in three-combination patterns. You have to learn one stance to be able to move to the next and then the next, creating techniques. Learning and mastering each technique then leads to a series of moves (putting them all together). This takes intense focus and uses short- and long-term memory, not to mention muscle memory. This was a perfect way to exercise Marston's memorizing capabilities while working his body, his strength, and core strength (balance).

We added a music appreciation class to his life skills curriculum. In this class, he learned to sing. We Weisses aren't natural-born singers, so it's safer to say they attempted to teach Marston to sing. He performed a song at the recital. He chose the Backstreet Boys' "I Want It That Way." He sang okay by that point. Still, he couldn't memorize all the words, like with the confirmation prayers, so he hummed where he'd lose track, then pick it back up. It was incredible to see him try so hard and sing loud enough for everyone to hear. What an accomplishment. Singing uses a different part of the brain. We figured—*let's work as much of that brain as possible!*

My favorite extracurricular activity was ballroom dancing. We thought for sure we were going to get turned down when we strutted into this professional studio asking if they'd take Marston on as a student. The head dance instructor, Ester, was this gorgeous, petite woman in her late twenties with a genuine *Dancing with the Stars* physique. She became Marston's private dance coach. He was mesmerized by her. She could have told him to go lie in the middle of the road all day, and he would have. And, Ester loved Marston back.

At the concert, she and Marston performed together to the original "James Bond Theme" song. The act started out with her tied up. Marston had to dance around her and help her escape. He shot a gun. They ultimately danced off into the sunset. The whole family came, including relatives. There wasn't a dry eye in the house. I was bawling my head off. Karin was, too. Marston shined like never before. He didn't have to speak, for one thing. He had rhythm and elegance out there on the dance floor with Ester. His attraction to her helped him focus and enhanced the performance. Plus, his stature and build made them look more like equals. You didn't notice the age difference too much. And you couldn't tell Marston wasn't like the other kids when he was dancing. I don't say this because Eric and I felt excited or relieved about Marston looking so normal; it's because Marston knew he looked good out there on the dance floor. He was the one who was excited and relieved. He felt like a so-called normal kid for an evening and exuded confidence. All eyes were on him, and no one strained to understand a story. No one asked him for a do-over. He was so happy.

Dancing helped with so many things. He got better at sequencing. He got to practice talking to a girl, over and over. Every practice was another opportunity to feel good about himself, thereby building his self-esteem.

They created a special award for him that evening: Most Improved.

He continued to dance for the next couple years. Ester eventually moved away to open her own studio in Kentucky. She is a saint, and I am forever indebted for her kindness and compassion.

13

I WISH THE WHOLE WORLD WAS LIKE THIS

"An autism mother does better research than the FBI."

—Anonymous
(My spin on: "A worried mother does better
research than the FBI.")

2013….

WHAT NEXT? MARSTON WAS EIGHTEEN when we knew his time with Karin was nearing the end. He was essentially homeschooled for the last several years, and it was time to become more independent. We decided to look for a place that could teach life skills and a vocation.

This meant it was time for more research.

We scoured the internet for potential schools. We hired an education consultant. And, as always, we prayed for Divine direction. Our search led us to a few schools, but we could not decide which would be best for Marston.

At this point in my life, my only respite was on the tennis court. A few hours of concentrating on a little, yellow ball, not ruminating on how to navigate the world of autism, was better than sedatives and cheaper than a psychiatrist. During this time, with Marston being older, I could go to the tennis court, bat a ball around, and think on my next best move for him.

We went to every school that had potential—we were parents touring "college campuses." Still, we couldn't figure out which one would be the best fit. The next day, on Monday, I was restless and knew I needed to make a decision. Luckily, it was also one of my tennis practice days—two hours of stress-free me time.

I got to the court early. I sat in the car and, once again, asked God to give me a sign—not for a tap on the shoulder, but a billboard (something I could not miss) to direct me to the perfect spot for Marston.

Upon entering the tennis facility, I was happy to discover I'd be playing with a woman I'd known since I was pregnant with Marston. As we were walking out to the court, Jill asked about my weekend. I told her about visiting Amenia, New York and the school there called Maplebrook. She laughed and responded she knew all about Maplebrook, as her sister had gone there thirty years earlier. After I reeled in my shock, I asked, "How don't I know this?"

Jill smiled and said, "I guess you never asked."

I had never known Jill had a special needs sister. In almost twenty years of friendship, she had never told me about her.

Then, she added, "Call my mom. She can tell you all about it."

I called her mom right after practice. She loved the Maplebrook environment, said the teachers were gentle, and the experience changed her daughter's life.

Jill's sister graduated from the school and went on to live independently. She was happier than she'd ever been after attending Maplebrook. I had asked God for a billboard and received all that plus peace of mind that Maplebrook was the place to send Marston. This God-whisper was immediate and still blows my mind today.

Maplebrook Postsecondary School in Amenia, New York was, in fact, the perfect place to put Marston's life skills into action in a community setting.

Maplebrook is a boarding school that was founded in the 1940s by three courageous women—Sunny Barlow, Serena Merck, and Marj Finger. These trailblazers in special needs education knew the brains of these kids did not work in the same way. Their vision in creating the school was to be able to capitalize on the strengths of unique learners, like Marston, and teach the skills of living.

This institute is fully accredited by the State of New York Board of Education. It's a highly structured, family-style environment where, upon graduation, students receive an actual high school diploma. Maplebrook is where students and teachers "do life together." This is how the kids learn to function interdependently and independently, how to make friends, how to have responsibility, how to become productive members of society, how to gain confidence. The school offers everything a regular high school would, such as art, theatre, chorus, regular academics, and athletics. Their athletic program is unique in that there are no tryouts. Everyone is required to participate in an activity every semester they're in attendance. They have so much to offer, from golf to soccer to equestrian to weights and fitness to cycling, skiing, basketball, etc.—it's pretty impressive. There is truly something for everyone. Marston would be attending the postsecondary program that teaches independent living and job skills, as well as academics.

A community of his peers living on a campus spanning across 100 acres in Upstate New York—this was going to be the next step in Marston's journey. The Maplebrook grounds are simply beautiful. They have dorm-style living but with an emphasis on independence. The institution comes with lots of rules. One of the big ones is sex is forbidden. There's zero tolerance.

Marston is a rule abider, thank goodness. But he was also a nineteen-year-old male that was going to be living among a lot of females in his age range.

When the boys were each in their early teens, Eric sat them both down for a six-week sex ed. training course. You wouldn't believe how much I learned! He taught them about the male anatomy, the female anatomy, and how everything works separately and together for the purposes of procreation and pleasure. They learned about the menstrual cycle and about both the male and female orgasms, including things like the male refractory period. Eric was so detailed. I am not kidding you. He taught them about birth control, venereal diseases, AIDS, and how to use a condom.

We've explained to Marston that he's not allowed to have sex until marriage, emphasizing that it goes against God's rules.

He tells us everything; he literally has no filter. So, we know he's never had sex. But, this is a legitimate concern of parents of autistic kids, or parents of any kids where the communication is not traditional when they are brain-injured. You want to protect your child and other people's children from the emotional and physical side effects of sexual intercourse. But, you can't be everywhere, and having sex is a natural part of becoming an adult for most people.

Also, we feel bad about the whole thing. Eric and I have had many conversations about this. These kids have already been denied so much by life. Life is not fair for special needs kids. But Marston isn't capable of being a father to a newborn, not on his own, and that's a fact. He deserves love. That's a fact, too. And he's capable of giving so much love. He's a grown man who's attracted to women. Do we give him a vasectomy? I mean, really; what do we do? How do we find a balance that will allow him to experience life to the fullest and keep us free from worrying?

Marston had a girlfriend while he was at Maplebrook. The majority of kids enrolled are legally adults. Not having sex at that age.... Well, do you remember that age? The good news for parents is that when you visit Maplebrook, you breathe a sigh of relief, as it feels more like a middle school environment over a college atmosphere. This is mainly because these kids haven't been exposed to regular adolescent environments and social situations like other kids. They're innocent. Nonetheless, they have attractions and urges, just like the rest of us.

Marston had been with his girlfriend for over a year during one of our visits when we were going over the Maplebrook code of ethics and, above all, God's moral code concerning intercourse.

He interrupted and counterpointed with "I've been praying about it, and I'm pretty sure God wants me to have sex."

God bless him, I could see his point.

He made it through Maplebrook abiding by the rules while learning to live independently. Some of the skills he learned or mastered included cleaning, cooking, laundry, hygiene, and driving. His romantic relationship didn't survive beyond his time there, though. That's part of growing up, too, for everyone.

With Marston living away from home, I had more time than ever to research. My brain was always in "what's next" mode. This led my warrior moms and me to a place called The Arc Village that was being built right in Jacksonville, Florida.

The Arc Jacksonville (Arc) is a nonprofit organization that has been championing the inclusion of persons with unique abilities, creating programs, and providing services since 1965. It was this organization that conceived of a place where adults with intellectual and developmental disabilities could live independently in order to achieve their full potential. In May 2016, the nation's first independent living community for adults with intellectual and developmental disabilities was opened. It was called the Villages and was erected on the Southside of Jacksonville, off Hodges Blvd. It housed 126 residents (its maximum capacity).

There was already a waiting list by 2014, two years before it was built. Eric and I put Marston on that list immediately. It was a longshot even then, but we got lucky. Marston won the lottery in 2015. We transferred him out of Maplebrook a year early so he'd be closer to home and into what we hoped would be a permanent adult environment. He's been living there ever since.

Whenever I visit, I think, *I wish the whole world was like this.* The people in the community are so nice to each other. They don't have another switch. They're just plain kind and sweet and thoughtful all the time. Marston lives in a one-bedroom, one-bath home by himself. In a gated community with thirty-eight separate homes, each resident has to be capable of living on their own with minimal supervision. Each resident has a mentor that checks on them several times a week.

I was hanging out with him at his home recently. He was playing *The Phantom of the Opera* soundtrack when there was a knock at the door.

I opened it and this girl entered.

"I heard your music. That's *Phantom*. I love that song."

He told her to sit down and listen with him. She did.

I told her my name was Chris and that I was Marston's mom.

She said, "Katey. Nice to meet you."

They talked about the music and some book they both liked. Then, without a word, she smiled, rose, and left his house.

I asked Marston, "How do you know Katey?"

He said, "I just met her. Like you just did."

Here's the thing about autism and communicating: a beginning is not required. It's just like with his stories. They'd start at the end or the middle, go forward and backward, and we'd often have to untangle them to get to the point or punchline. Most of the conversations I've witnessed between Marston and other similarly challenged people all take place "somewhere in the middle." It's efficient, that's for sure. They get to the meat of the conversation, to the point. Then, when that's been established, they're done.

In many ways, it's admirable. It sure takes the guesswork out of relationships.

.º .º .º.

As of this writing, Marston attends the University of North Florida. He's enrolled in their **On Campus Transition** program for kids with unique intellectual needs.

In 2007, ARC partnered with the University of North Florida (UNF) to create an innovative program so kids like Marston can have a transformational college experience as an integral part of their transition to independence. Students participate in all aspects of college life through On Campus Transition (OCT) by auditing UNF courses, joining campus organizations and clubs, and participating in recreational/leisure activities that are enjoyed by all UNF students. Students are mentored in academic, social, and recreational activities through mentoring programs with UNF student peers.

Some of the classes he's audited include: Music Appreciation, Theater Appreciation, History of the US WWI to Present, Golf, and Greek Mythology.

Marston works on campus in one of their restaurants, a coffee shop/pizzeria. He's been there since 2016.

Marston has come so far. We were lucky that he was born in a "good mood"; I've been thanking God for that every day. His disposition is just like Eric's; they are both so sweet, they're always happy, and they're people pleasers. As an adult, Marston has zero sensory issues. I believe that's thanks to all the programs, starting with the strict curriculum from the IAHP and Sensory Learning. He's social. That could be because we tossed him over and over into social situations, especially with all of Austin's sports. I couldn't leave Marston at home, and I wasn't going to miss Austin's baseball games. I think Marston learned to adapt in many situations all on his own, through years of observance. If I had to sum up his hard work with one word, it would be repetition.

Like the world-class athlete, the pianist, the inventor, the singer, the painter, the public speaker, the surgeon, Marston practiced every minute of his waking life, and sometimes in his sleep, to perfect his dream and achieve his goal of being a caring, intelligent, self-sufficient, conscientious, content human to the best of his ability.

PART II

Stem Cell Replacement Therapy

14

THE SCIENCE BEHIND STEM CELLS

—2016—

I WAS IN TARGET WHEN I got a tap on the shoulder. It was my friend, Brenda, the woman who walked the Camino de Santiago with me. Her son and former daughter-in-law have a child with autism. She had asked me to call and help her with ideas for therapy, and for moral support in general. I was in fairly regular contact via email but hadn't reached out in a while.

"Chris, I forgot to tell you, Christy went to Panama for stem cell therapy treatments!" she blurted in the checkout line as I turned to face her.

I listened to the story, but, for some reason, it didn't resonate. It may have been the "she went to Panama" part, or maybe I was narrowly thinking that if the therapy was that good, somebody reputable would be doing it in the United States. Anyway, after the conversation, I got in my car, not giving it another thought.

When I got home, I got a ping on my phone. The text was from Eric's IT guy, Remo. He was this really sweet, smart Jamaican guy who had a beautiful nature about him. From the minute we met, I liked him. He knew about our struggles with helping Marston navigate the world. Remo texted me a YouTube link about umbilical cord stem cells and autism. It was a video of a lecture by the same doctor in Panama that Brenda had just mentioned an hour earlier in Target.

What are the chances?

I had completely missed the tap on the shoulder, but I was not going to miss this. (God must know I need billboards.) I watched the video and sent it to Eric. Now, I was excited about the possibility of stem cell therapy. For starters, we hadn't tried it, and, by this point, there wasn't much on our "haven't tried" list.

Eric first studied stem cells and their healing potential thirty years ago during his residency in California. Stem cells have also been a hot topic in the field of plastic surgery, his area of practice, for the last quarter of a century. Using stem cells to heal Marston's brain has been on Eric's mind since Marston was officially diagnosed with autism when he was four.

This is where I'm going to step back and let Eric take over, as we embark on our journey to understand stem cells and how they could work to heal Marston's brain.

ERIC

On Chris's prompting, I watched the video, made notes, and downloaded Dr. Neil Riordan's book *Stem Cell Therapy: A Rising Tide: How Stem Cells Are Disrupting Medicine and Transforming Lives*. Then, I sent him an email. (I highly recommend this book. It's an accessible read for anyone interested in learning more about stem cell therapy.)

Dr. Neil Riordan is an American scientist who has been studying stem cells and their potential healing effects for decades. His main focus has been on degenerative diseases and autism. His laboratory is located in Panama, as there is more freedom in stem cell research there. (The FDA has placed many restrictions on the harvesting, manipulation, and clinical use of stem cells in the United States.) Dr. Riordan is an expert on the beneficial effects that stem cells can have on a variety of human diseases and conditions.

In order to understand the possibility of this game-changing therapy, it's vital to understand stem cells.

How Stem Cells Work:

This can be a very detailed and complex discussion, but I will try to leave as much cellular biology out as possible, while still explaining medically why stem cell therapy may be important in treating autism. I will start out with the big picture: What are stem cells? How do they work? And, then I will explain why they can play an important role in helping both children and adults with autism.

As with many great medical stories, it all started in a lab. So there would be no risk of rejection, researchers studying aging took two genetically identical mice (one old and one young) and connected them surgically. This essentially made them "'Siamese twins"—two mice with one circulatory system. This is called heterochromic parabiosis. They discovered that, in uniting their vascular systems, the older rat became physiologically younger, while the younger rat became physiologically older. What is in the blood of the young rat that keeps them young? What is lacking in older rats but is introduced through this process to make their bodies behave younger?

This simple experiment was pivotal in discovering, defining, and understanding the role of stem cells.

Stem cells are defined as cells that are "pluripotent," meaning that unlike other cells that divide to make identical copies of themselves, stem cells can make multiple cell types. That is, one type of stem cell can divide to make skin, muscle, cartilage, bone, or nerve cells. Quite amazing. The other fascinating quality stem cells possess is the ability to transmit messages to other cells for the purpose of repair. They do this by secreting tiny packets of information called exosomes that can travel throughout the body to a target cell. This target cell then absorbs the exosome (the tiny packet of information). The exosome has all sorts of proteins that

150

stimulate the target cell to divide or perform any number of other activities that need to be done to fix the problem the stem cell (that released this packet) has recognized.

Summary: Stem cells can divide to make any cell in the body, and through the release of exosomes, they can regulate that cell's behavior.

Most people think of embryonic stem cells when they first hear the term stem cells. Embryonic stem cells are pluripotent (master) stem cells derived from an early-stage embryo. They're able to make all cells necessary for life, so they can "potentially" produce any cell or tissue the body needs to repair itself. These cells, taken from a developing fetus early in cellular division, sound ideal. But, multiple studies have demonstrated their propensity to form tumors. Additionally, **there are** significant ethical concerns surrounding the use of stem cells from a once-living being whose life was aborted (I concur with these concerns); that, along with restricted access to these cells, have limited their use for routine clinical application in patients.

These embryonic stem cells are not the type of stem cells we are talking about. Adult stem cells are the type of stem cells most useful in the treatment of autism spectrum disorder and other various diseases. There is some confusion, as most people associate adult stem cells with adults or mature individuals; however, even a fetus has adult stem cells. These adult stem cells originate from embryonic stem cells and are just further down the developmental pathway, more specialized and limited in what they can make.

There are several types of adult stem cells, each with their own specialization in what cells they can make and what cells they can influence. The major types of adult stem cells include:

- **Mesenchymal Stem Cell**: capable of making skin, muscle, bone, cartilage
- **Hematopoetic Stem Cell**: capable of making all components of the blood and immune system
- **Neuro Stem Cell**: capable of making neurons and neuron-supporting cells
- **Endothelial Stem Cell**: capable of making blood vessels
- **Epithelial Stem Cell**: capable of making the gut

The main job of adult stem cells is to repair, restore, and maintain normal body function. They are constantly on guard to fix cells, tissue, and organs that are not working properly, whether due to trauma, a disorder, disease, or just age. These cells can be found in humans of all ages and are most prominent in the bone marrow and peripheral fat. However, there is a much greater quantity in the umbilical cord and in umbilical cord blood.

Summary: Adult Stem Cells are not Embryonic Stem Cells. Adult Stem Cells aid in restoring and maintaining function

and are found in greatest number in the umbilical cord and umbilical cord blood.

All cells in the body have a defined lifespan. Once this is reached, the cell dies by a process termed "apoptosis" or "programed cell death." These cells are then replaced by new cells. These new cells are the products of stem cells. Our bodies' own adult stem cells are located throughout the body and aid in cell replacement after apoptosis and injury. This is one of the definitions of aging—where the process of cellular death outpaces the body's ability to produce new cells.

These stem cells are also always vigilant for injuries, and they aid in recovery and tissue repair. The problem is our stem cells also have a defined lifespan, and they age out. By the end of the teenage years, approximately 90 percent of these cells are gone. By our mid-thirties, 95 percent are gone. By our mid-fifties, 98 percent, and, by our eighties, 99 percent are gone. This is why, as you age, your ability to recovery from surgery or injury decreases significantly, and the likelihood of degenerative diseases and illnesses increase.

The progress made in science and medicine in the last several decades has significantly improved healthcare, increased the quality of life, and extended lifespans. Unfortunately, a variety of factors in our daily life, such as urbanization, aging of the population, exposure to toxins, tobacco, alcohol abuse, inappropriate diets, and sedentary lifestyles have caused an increase in the number of people suffering from cardiovascular, neurological, neurodegenerative, osteoarthritis, and diabetic conditions. Most of these affect the normal lifespan, resulting in invalidity, requiring lifelong care of symptoms and systematic treatment, as well as having an enormous impact on a person's family and financial situation. Therefore, current research is focused on degenerative disorders, the common factor of which is the dysfunction and death of the central cell types.

As I said before, one source of adult stem cells is exists in our own growing and aging bodies. We have discovered that bone marrow and peripheral fat have rich sources of adult stem cells. These sources contain both hematopoietic stem cells (HSCs) and mesenchymal stem cells (MSCs). HSCs are responsible for the formation of all of the elements of the blood/immune system, while MSCs are responsible for bone, skin, cartilage, and nerve tissue. These stem cells essentially wait for something bad to happen. Once there is an injury, they are called to the site or called to secrete factors by a very complex chemical pathway—that scientists are only beginning to understand—and start the healing process. Unfortunately, we do not have an unlimited supply of these mesenchymal stem cells. If we did, stem cell therapy wouldn't be necessary, as the body would continually make its own. Multiple studies have demonstrated that one can harvest these cells, isolate them, and use them to treat multiple orthopedic ailments.

Another source, and potentially the greatest source of stem cells, is the umbilical cord. Both the umbilical cord blood and Wharton's Jelly (gelatinous tissue inside the lining of the cord) have been shown to harbor vast quantities of stem cells. Cells that are found here include HSCs, MSCs, endothelial stem cells, epithelial stem cells, unrestricted somatic stem cells, as well as multiple T and B white blood cells, including a subpopulation termed T regulatory cells. These umbilical cord stem cells are like the ones found in older people; however, they have three unique properties. The first is they have the ability to replicate 1,000 trillion times and differentiate into a much wider cell population than the HSCs and MSCs found in bone and fat. If one takes a stem cell from a person in their mid-fifties, puts it in a Petri dish, and stimulates it to divide, at the end of thirty days, there might be a thousand cells. If one takes an umbilical cord blood stem cell and stimulates it to divide, at the end of thirty days, there will be over a billion cells.

The second unique property is that umbilical stem cells are immunologically privileged, meaning they do not express self-proteins. These umbilical cord blood stem cells are generic stem cells and can be given to anybody without fear of rejection or another issue called graft-versus-host disease.

The third quality of umbilical cord blood stem cells is they can secrete a vast number of exosomes that are uniquely made for a multitude of issues. These packets of information—which are created in response to multiple ongoing issues in the body—are released, find their way to problem, and begin to fix it. The younger the stem cell, the greater quantity and variety of exosomes that can be made to repair issues in the body.

The umbilical cord stem cells' abilities to replicate, their vast differential and exosome capabilities, and their ability to be given across HLA antigens (this is what gets "matched" in a kidney or liver transplant) make them uniquely qualified to be used clinically.

The scientific research community used to think these transplanted stem cells would migrate to the area of disease or injury and turn into whatever cell was needed. These cells have been shown to be effective in repairing the heart after a heart attack or the brain after a stroke. Therefore, researchers assumed the stem cells migrated to the heart or brain and started making cardiac or brain cells—essentially whatever was needed.

This proved not to be the case. New research has shown, and current thinking is, that the transplanted stem cells take up a position close to (or even sometimes far away from) the injury or issue. They then begin to secrete exosomes that travel to the area of injury, become incorporated, and stimulate the local cell to begin the healing process. The message contained in the exosomes actually turns on the regenerative capacity of the injured cell to heal itself. If we remember our two mice that were connected, it was the exosomes traveling from the young mouse to the old that turned on the regenerative capacity that was absent due to age.

Summary: The umbilical cord and umbilical cord blood stem cells are unique in their ability to divide and to secrete a much broader spectrum of exosomes and can be transplanted

into anyone. They have much more healing potential than stem cells harvested from fat or bone marrow.

I will skip over all the other indicators for stem cells. I will now completely focus on autism and how stem cells have helped my child.

Autism spectrum disorder is a neurodevelopmental disorder characterized by impairment in social communication, the presence of repetitive behavior, and a restricted range of behavior, with onset early in life. Treatment approaches include medication, behavioral therapy, occupational and speech therapy, and specialized educational and vocational support. All currently available therapies are intended to manage some symptoms or behaviors but do not address core autism physiologic abnormalities or causes. The cause remains unknown despite evidence that genetic, environmental, and immunological factors may play a role in its pathogenesis.

The genetic predisposition to ASD is still being worked out; there are multiple candidates, but no dominant genetic defect that leads to autism has been discovered. Growing research has highlighted maternal immune activation (MIA), especially during the first or second trimester of pregnancy, as one potential environmental factor. Evidence shows that bacterial or viral infection during this critical time is associated with increased risk of ASD. Season of birth is important. Women who experience the first trimester during the winter months are associated with increased rates of ASD. This role of inflammation in the mother is further boosted by epidemiologic data from large populations showing increased rates of autoimmune disorder in the family of children with ASD.

Inflammation, and specifically the role of neuroinflammation (brain inflammation) of those affected by autism, is being researched more extensively. A key finding in ASD research has been the observation of marked, ongoing neuroinflammation in autopsy brain specimens from individuals with ASD over a wide range of ages. These studies look at the brains of ASD children and adults who died of unrelated causes (a car accident, for example). Ages range from five to forty-five years old.

The vast majority have significant, ongoing inflammation. The findings included prominent microglial activation and increased inflammatory cytokines (chemicals released by certain cells that promote inflammation) in both the brain tissue and cerebral spinal fluid. Speaking plainly, **microglia** are **key cells** in overall brain maintenance. They hunt plaques, damaged or unnecessary neurons and synapses, and other infectious agents—and they eradicate the damaged cells through phagocytosis or by releasing cytokines. (The discovery of excess microglial activation and increase in inflammatory cytokines are important in understanding how stem cells may work.)

In addition to this central nerve inflammation, multiple studies demonstrate peripheral systemic inflammation. Other studies

158

indicate that the levels of many immune proteins in the plasma, such as cytokines, chemokines, complement proteins, adhesion molecules, and growth factors, are altered in ASD. This data all points to a proinflammatory state in these individuals. The immune response is also affected with decreased activity of NK (natural killer) cells and monocytes.

Although a singular pathology of ASD remains elusive, a wealth of evidence suggests that ASD symptoms may be related to immune dysfunction. Activity of the immune system can elicit profound effects and behaviors. All these inflammatory chemicals can lead to social withdrawal, impaired cognition, and repetitive behaviors in multiple animal models—all seen in ASD.

Umbilical cord blood is rich in MSCs. These MSCs, when given in experimental models of inflammation (i.e., neuroinflammation), have been shown to have the ability to decrease or eliminate inflammation. These cells do not all head to the brain and replace damaged neurons, but they "set up" in the body. They have the ability to read these inflammatory mediators and then start to divide and produce exosomes. These exosomes can travel from the stem cells through the body system across the blood-brain barrier—which prevents dangerous proteins in the blood from affecting the brain—and fuse with the microglial cells. This information then causes the cells' DNA/RNA to turn off the inflammation and start the restorative process.

These exosomes also work on peripheral inflammation. The stem cells have the ability to decipher the complex inflammatory signals of the body and brain, make specific exosomes for each cell, and release them to find their specific home. All this results in decreased inflammation and more normal function, allowing the body to heal itself.

I do believe stem cells will help the majority of patients with ASD. However, whatever the cause of autism—and there may be many—I believe the common pathway may be neuroinflammation. All other therapies—behavioral and medicinal—will take a backseat and will be less effective until the neuroinflammation is turned off.

Stem cell therapy studies are being done on people with MS, traumatic brain injuries, and infectious diseases. Autism is now on that growing list. This is essentially a transplant, but, as mentioned, unlike any other transplant, anti-rejection drugs are not needed. (Umbilical cord stem cells are immune privileged, meaning the body does not recognize them as foreign, so they can live in the body without the fear of rejection.)

But, because our stem cell supply not only depletes with age but loses the ability to divide quickly to repair tissue before irreversible scarring takes place, we need young stem cells. It comes down to numbers.

As it turns out, the umbilical cord and the cord blood from live, healthy babies—something that is discarded thousands of times daily—has a rich supply of these early MSCs. In fact, the umbilical cord stem cells lack the usual protein coating that causes an adverse immune reaction because they are so new and regenerate so quickly. This is the reason there's no need for a donor match, as these cells can be given to anyone for any condition, disease, or disorder that needs to be treated. This makes them immensely usable in medical care.

The ability of the umbilical cord stem cells to replicate is amazing. The downside: it takes many cords to get enough MSCs to be of use clinically. On top of that, breakthroughs in stem cell research had been occurring in foreign countries, but not so much in the United States. This essentially came down to FDA restrictions on certain types of research, which prevented the ability to generate the large numbers of stem cells needed in these types of experiments.

In other countries, such as Panama and China, researchers are allowed to clone the MSCs in a Petri dish, generating millions, if not billions, from one cord. This makes research and clinical use a breeze. The FDA feels, however, that when you stimulate the MSCs to grow outside the body, it may cause a malignant mutation that is potentially cancerous. Every time a cell divides, there is a potential risk of DNA damage causing a malignancy. These cells are artificially stimulated to divide billions of times; this increases the risk of a cancer-causing mutation. If these cells are then unknowingly transplanted into a patient, cancer could form.

Fortunately, thanks to a few scientists who have devoted their careers to stem cell extraction and use (and thanks to their investors), there are currently several laboratories in the United States that have developed the technology to harvest, wash, and freeze umbilical cord blood, so the healing properties can be banked for later use. They have been licensed by the FDA to extract MSCs from umbilical cords and cord blood to aid in tissue repair. The first use was in the treatment of childhood leukemia.

As Chris mentioned, I already knew a fair amount about stem cells before she told me about Dr. Riordan—from my residency and because of my area of expertise. Plastic surgeons all over the country and world were trying to define the exact mechanism of wound healing, tissue repair, and tissue regeneration.

In our collective, personal studies of this process since around 2015, Chris and I started to note that research had begun (though not in the United States) into the potential benefits of umbilical cord stem cells for children with autism. We were both initially skeptical, as you can imagine. But, on becoming reacquainted with the potential benefits of stem cells, thanks to a tap on the shoulder in Target and Dr. Neil Riordan's research and book, we decided to start the process of verification.

15

STEM CELL THERAPY OPTIONS
FOR MARSTON

—2017—

HAVING FINISHED DR. RIORDAN'S BOOK and about a 100 more articles on the subject, I was inspired by the potential of stem cell therapy. And, I believed two things were certain: umbilical stem cells were safe, and they offered the possibility of benefit. Still, trying to find a study that used adults as their subjects, well, that seemed nonexistent.

If one googles stem cells and autism now, multiple hits come up. But, even as recently as 2017, this wasn't the case. It took some digging. I found and evaluated several clinics, but none were to my liking. Many were chiropractors or ER physicians working for a company. It was sometimes difficult to discern whether I was talking to a physician or a salesman.

I contacted the medical library at the University of Florida to do a literature search on all things stem cells and any other books or articles Riordan had authored or co-written that I may have overlooked in the last year. Chris found a Duke article on the subject. The "investigators" demonstrated that there were sound physiologic principles and clinical evidence to believe umbilical cord stem cells could help with a multitude of medical issues, including autism.

Duke University researchers had seen benefits of using umbilical cord stem cells in autistic children. Because I went to Duke for medical school, I knew many of the doctors still on staff, as well as people in high places—not to mention, I had the phone number to the hospital memorized. I called them and asked for Dr. Kurtzberg or Dr. Sun. Both were unavailable, but I was informed they would call me back. Many times, this is a blow-off, but not with this group.

A day later, Dr. Jessica Sun called me back. We had a fascinating and thorough discussion about their research and new phase II study for kids under the age of eight. Dr. Sun was encouraging and said they had seen some unbelievable improvements and felt Marston could really benefit if I could find a clinic willing to treat him.

"I know exactly who to call," was Chris's response to the news that Marston was too old to qualify for the study.

Her friend had a child with autism who was seven at this time. To say she was excited to hear about a stem cell study that may benefit her son was an understatement. Every new study increases the chances for a breakthrough. Every individual win in the fight against autism is a win for everyone.

I contacted Dr. Riordan and his researchers in Panama again.

They were excluding anybody with autism over the age of eighteen for their current protocol. During the conversation, I asked if they implemented the age restriction due to data that suggested older kids did not benefit from the treatment. The answer was no; it was an arbitrary cutoff with no scientific basis. The goal now was to find a doctor willing to give Marston umbilical cord stem cells.

While I researched further and contacted fellow doctors all over the country, Chris asked her friend, Christy (whose son was already obtaining treatments in Panama), to put the word out on her autism moms Facebook group chats. A doctor in Chicago was mentioned as a possibility: Thomas Lobe, MD.

(By this time, Christy and her family had witnessed definite results from the first stem cell replacement therapy treatment and had more lined up.)

I went to Dr. Lobe's website and immediately liked what I saw. He was a surgeon like me, with very similar training. He is a pediatric surgeon; I am a plastic surgeon. We both had completed general surgery residencies. He spent time at UCLA, while I was a few hours north, in San Francisco. He'd been the head of pediatric surgery at St. Jude Children's Hospital for twenty years, a remarkable accomplishment.

I phoned him. His office said he'd call me back when he was done with the day's surgeries. It was perfect, exactly what I do: operate all day, make phone calls at night.

Dr. Lobe called me back about 5:30 p.m. my time. I was leaving the office and took the call on the ride home. We were still talking when I walked in the door, forty-five minutes later.

We felt convinced we had either met before or knew the same people. In addition to similar training, we discussed surgery, life, Marston, stem cells, and autism. We had connected through our desire to help people and our training and found we did have friends in common. I will always remember how friendly and eager to help he was. Dr. Lobe had said he'd personally seen amazing healing and advances with stem cell therapy. Then, he told me that he'd try stem cell replacement therapy in a heartbeat if Marston were his son. He offered to administer the cells to Marston personally.

When you have an autistic child or a child with any kind of special needs for which there isn't a cure, you'll do anything, try anything, spend any amount of money in the hopes that you can heal them. Chris's initial reaction to any new therapy or treatment or medicine was always: "I'll grab the checkbook and pack our bags!" But, there are a lot of snake oil salesmen out there. And, sometimes, all you have to go on is a feeling.

It's luck, really. I'm fortunate that I'm in the field I'm in, given my son's circumstances. I have access to doctors every day. In addition, I speak the language and can differentiate between the real deals and the snake oil salesmen. I've always had a sixth sense about integrity, and I felt great about Dr. Lobe from Chicago.

I shared the news with Chris. We made an appointment and set up the first stem cell transfusion for Marston.

I'd been waiting twenty years for technology to catch up. I've always believed stem cell therapy was the key to healing Marston, and Chris agreed.

And, now, it was going to happen.

16

MARSTON'S FIRST TRANSFUSION

I WAS AT UCSF (UNIVERSITY of California, San Francisco) in the late eighties for my general surgery residency. During that time, there were some incredible discoveries centered on fetal wound healing: the potential to heal adults like the fetus heals in the womb. Early in the pregnancy, the fetus heals by regeneration, not scarring.

Early on, when we knew for certain there was an "issue" with Marston, I knew it was anatomic. I knew he was lacking white matter, and I just felt like his brain could be fixed. I've always felt this was the key to making Marston whole. I knew we needed some way to unlock the healing potential of stem cells, so they could heal his brain through regeneration. But, doctors were not talking about this back in the day, in the late eighties or early nineties. I'd had a couple seminal moments, however, and they had stuck with me.

The first happened when I was at a trauma center in California during my internship. I took care of a young kid on a Saturday afternoon. He was on a track scholarship at a local college. He was running when one of the athletes competing in a field event threw the hammer outside the designated perimeter. It hit him and crushed his skull. (The hammer is a sixteen-pound metal ball on a wire. It's swung around and around and propelled through the air with two hands and by centripetal force.) I called neurosurgeons. They said they'd be there in five and told me to get the kid into the OR and shave his head. I did that, they arrived, and then I went into the waiting area and told his folks he was in good hands.

The surgeons removed almost a third of his brain, as it had been irreversibly injured with the trauma. I followed along until he got transferred in a vegetative state to a long-term facility.

So, the *San Francisco Chronicle* used to have pages dyed green in their Sunday addition called the green pages—it was the sports section. This brings me to a few years later….

I was reading the green pages, and one of the articles read that John Doe (we did not focus on anyone's name in the ER, and I can't recall his real name from back then or from the paper), who had suffered a traumatic brain injury from having his skull crushed by a hammer during a track meet, had just graduated from college with his bachelor's degree. He had awakened after being comatose for two months and went back to school like it had never happened.

I couldn't believe it. I contacted the neurosurgeon team, and they confirmed the report. He woke up from his coma after several months and, with therapy, progressively improved—talking, walking, etc. He improved to the point of having minimal disability from the devastating sports accident that had destroyed a third of his brain.

A story like that gets stored in your memory bank, and it moves to the forefront of your consciousness when you realize someone you love has a brain injury. *If a guy with two thirds of a brain can recover, then why can't I fix my son?* The plasticity of the brain, its ability to heal itself, is related to stem cells. I was exposed to it every single day as a general surgery resident. And, I was witness to the miracle of the brain's plasticity with the young track star.

If this kid could live a full and normal life, my son could be healed—for he has a whole brain.

March 2018

I remember several things about Marston's first stem cell transfusion. The first was that it was somewhat anticlimactic, not like a liver or kidney transplant.

I was used to the process of harvesting an organ from a brain-dead individual, packing it in ice, and jet-transferring it to the recipient. Meanwhile, the other surgeon is waiting on standby. The new organ arrives, and the delicate, time-sensitive procedure begins. The ineffective organ is removed from the recipient, the new one goes in. After that, there's blood loss, and the patient is sick and in a healing crisis. They're moved to the intensive care unit as we wait for the new organ to function, for the patient to show signs of recovery, and for the immunosuppressive medication to do its job. We set up camp, ever-vigilantly hoping the recipient's system does not reject the new intruder.

None of this happens with stem cells. Mannitol is given several minutes prior to open the blood-brain barrier so the stem cells can pass through. Then, during the procedure, stem cells are infused over a matter of fifteen to twenty seconds. Boom. Done.

There's none of the excitement or worry of an organ transplant. And, remember, these stem cells are immune privileged, so there is no worry of rejection.

The second thing I remember is the day after the infusion.

Chris, Marston, and I were in the café in the hotel lobby for breakfast.

After we exchanged morning pleasantries, got comfortable, and ordered, Marston asked, "How did you two meet?"

"We came down here five minutes ago, honey, and grabbed a couple coffees while we were waiting for you," Chris replied.

"No, I mean, how did you two meet for the first time?"

Marston had never asked us a single question about our history. Marston has never asked any questions that weren't "immediate" or didn't illicit easy responses. *Is it warm out today? How do I make salsa?* Heck, I can't recall Austin or William ever asking Chris and me how we met. He stopped us in our tracks with this one.

After Chris and I walked down memory lane to Marston's satisfaction, he smiled, and breakfast arrived.

We dug in. As he was pouring syrup on his waffles, he then asked, "Where does maple syrup come from?"

For Marston, and many kids like Marston, wondering about the derivation of maple syrup or peanut butter or popcorn is not part of their cognitive process. Maple syrup is just that: it's maple syrup, just like the sky is blue and cars transport us on roads from here to there.

We were firsthand witnesses to the miracle of stem cell therapy. Marston was much more inquisitive.

He became more conversational, clearer, more independent, better at time management, etc.

We were convinced that giving stem cells via umbilical cord blood is safe; it is a logical treatment option that can be supported by basic science and clinical evidence and offers the hope of significant benefit.

These results led to setting up a second treatment.

17

MORE EVIDENCE ON THE POTENTIAL OF STEM CELLS

BACK AT MY PRACTICE, I'D been treating a sixty-eight-year-old woman who had severe hidradenitis suppurativa of the groin. Let's call her "Gail." This is a chronic, bacterial infection that is impossible to treat with antibiotics. The affected flesh needs to be cut out and removed from the body or it will spread. Suppurativa is literally flesh-eating bacteria. Gail was sick, debilitated, and unable to work. She'd been in a wheelchair as long as I'd known her due to her condition.

Her surgeries were lifesaving but deforming, as they involved cutting out skin and fat. The infection was attacking her bottom, groin, pubic area, etc. I ended up cutting almost everything away, from her navel to her buttocks, her labia, glutes, and more. She was debilitated and malnourished and appeared older than her age.

After getting her through the final operation, it was time for the reconstruction. This would be difficult, at best. I'd been contemplating surgical options for a while. I remembered an article I'd read several months earlier about a stem cell product used in lower extremity reconstruction. And, I'd heard about the cords being used to heal the feet of diabetics after chunks of flesh had been destroyed and removed. I thought it offered a chance to heal with the lowest complications possible.

May 2018

After making sure the hospital would obtain the product, I booked the case. The sales rep was overjoyed that I knew about the product and had a new indication for how it could be used. The product is called Amniox and is made by TissueTech. It's a cryopreserved umbilical cord on an amniotic membrane matrix. It is kept frozen until ready for use. So, it's just sitting there "on ice" at their facility—and it can sit there only so long before they have to discard it.

Upon receiving the biologic tissue, the clock started ticking. Gail was already asleep, prepped, and draped by the time I started cutting the cord into strips. Then, I stuck these strips into the wounds all over her torso, genital area, and buttocks. I bandaged them all carefully with gauze and sent her to the nursing home.

And that was it.

For the first few weeks, the strips just lay there, doing nothing, neither hurting nor helping these open wounds.

We needed more time.

Two or three months after that, she walked into my office. It was the first time she'd walked without assistance in years.

She was completely healed. Not only that, but the affected regions contained 95 percent new tissue, and only about 5 percent of her skin had scarring. The umbilical cord stem cells had programmed her body to regenerate healthy skin cells.

This was my first venture into using stem cells for healing. It was a straight-up miracle. I truly could not believe it.

I took pictures to show Amniox the results and got a nice reply when I sent them.

Two days later, an orthopedic surgeon called me. It turned out we had been in the Navy together. The company had forwarded the photos to him. He was amazed at the healing potential of the stem cells. He was giving a lecture on lower extremity wounds in a couple days and asked permission to use my patient and the photos in his talk. I said, "Certainly." The word needed to get out on the healing potential of these cells.

So, at this point, I was witness to the amazing healing effects of utilizing stem cells—not only on my son, but also in my clinical practice of plastic surgery.

This was the tipping point to the life-altering decision we'd been considering for over a year.

If You're Wondering How It Works:

The umbilical cord connects mom to baby. It's a biological connection from one individual to another. We know this is a unique situation. (We know in the case of organ transplants, it makes sense to give anti-rejection drugs.) However, with an umbilical cord, the normal proteins on the outside of cells, which determine "self," are not present. These are generic cells, and they are the reason umbilical cord blood and stem cells can be transplanted without fear of rejection. This is kind of cool on God's part. He's amazing. The cord cells are free to be used in anyone who needs them. There are ten times as many stem cells in umbilical cord blood as there are in the bone marrow of people under fifty. And, if you recall, by our mid-fifties, our stem cells are all but done regenerating (98 percent gone) and have a shorter lifespan— one year. These are just a few of the reasons this process is delicate, pricey, and tedious.

(By the way: generic cells from "Baby Jane" get tested for over 130 diseases to make sure they are okay prior to medical use in the US.)

In the case of Gail, the sixty-eight-year-old woman I bandaged the umbilical cord strips to, she was completely healed in about three months. But, according to research, it typically takes longer.

Now, I'd made a bunch of connections. Marston was seeing results from his stem cell transfusion, and I had had one successful experience with stem cells under my belt as a physician. By this point, Marston was getting ready for his second session with Dr. Lobe.

At this time, I had a great conversation with Dr. Lobe about his clinic and how stem cells are improving the lives of his pediatric patients and adults alike. That's when he told me about Stemell, the source of his supply.

18

STEMELL

IF WE TRULY BELIEVED IN these cells, then why not offer this therapy as a part of my practice? I couldn't get this thought out of my head.

Well, there were plenty of why nots.

First, we have a thriving plastic surgery practice. I already feel like I work as hard as I can. Second, as a plastic surgeon, all you have is your reputation; when you venture out into something new, you leave yourself vulnerable for criticism, not only by lay people but by other plastic surgeons. I would need to hire staff, train others, and develop new marketing material. This would involve a commitment of time, energy, and money. I already do not see enough of my wife…. Luckily, she was on board and helped with the process.

The first thing I did was attempt to read all significant scientific articles about stem cells as they pertain to regenerative medicine in general from the last five years. This led to many volumes of bound notebooks and an even greater relationship with the medical librarian at the University of Florida.

After more intensive reading and note taking, I became convinced there are sound scientific principles by which to believe umbilical cord stem cells could help a variety of disorders. There is significant experimental and clinical evidence that these umbilical cord stem cells can help patients recover from strokes, traumatic brain injuries, heart attacks, liver disease, diabetes, chronic traumatic (brain) encephalopathy, cerebral palsy, and, of course, autism. I want to be able to defend any clinical decision I make. I can inform patients on what is known and unknown, and what to expect.

Now that I was comfortable with the concept, I needed to find a lab that would supply the cells. There were a handful to choose from. After reading available literature, visiting websites, and looking at viability data, I decided that, like Dr. Lobe, I would choose Stemell in San Juan Capistrano, California.

The industry standard for cell viability after harvest, cleaning, separation, and freezing was between 40–60 percent, meaning that only 40–60 percent of the cells that I was going to be infusing into a patient would actually be alive. Stemell data was far superior. Independent, third-party verification demonstrated their cells average 92 percent viability. Getting the cord blood and purifying the cells is Stemell's specialty. From harvest to delivery, this clinic is light-years ahead of other labs in the United States.

This led to me calling, and eventually talking to, Peyman Taeidi, the president of Stemell. His education and reputation are topnotch. He is a PhD in cellular biology with an emphasis on cellular communication in stem cell biology. He studied at the University of Tehran as well as the University of California, Irvine. He has written multiple scientific articles focusing on stem cells, and cells in general. This education led to practical experiments; he was a senior scientist at multiple major corporations and government labs, like Johnson & Johnson, Cytori Therapeutics, Prodo Labs, the Department of Homeland Security, Pfizer, and Eli Lilly. A passion for science, coupled with zeal to make medical care easier for patients, drove him to start Stemell.

As soon as I'd heard he had been affiliated with Cytori Therapeutics, I felt like I could vet him effectively. Two surgeons affiliated with Cytori had been in my residency program at UCSF. These were guys I had worked closely with, had gone through the war with; I would take a bullet for them, and they would for me. It is like in the movies and TV—at least they get that part of residency right. We work long hours, get minimal sleep and food, and form a brotherhood to survive. I called each of my buddies. They both said

Peyman was brilliant, hardworking, and extremely ethical. That was all I needed to continue my investigation.

A few days later, I called Peyman back to set up a site visit. We wanted to see the labs and meet him and the staff. The meeting went extremely well.

Stemell was everything we'd imagined and more: a state-of-the-art facility that was compliant with all federal and state regulations. It had an aggressive quality assurance program, and everybody employed there had the drive to deliver a better product. Peyman assisted with many of the protocols and processes involved in procurement, removing unwanted cells, and concentrating the ones that were needed. This is why his viability is much better than the industry average. (The FDA is currently working with him to make some of his work industry standard.)

Peymen even developed his packaging, which is a closed system to decrease the risk of contamination. He built the machine that packages his cells.

After the tour and talk, I was more excited than ever.

Chris and I went to dinner with him and his wife, Bennie, that evening. They were a beautiful couple dedicated to their work and desire to improve the lives of the sick. We knew Peyman was the right guy to help us move forward in healing Marston. We'd been guided to him.

Right at dinner, we told him we wanted to work in this field and gain the knowledge he already had. Chris and I were eager to attend some conferences on stem cells and learn everything we could.

Somewhere along the way, I realized he was interviewing me, too. I had done my homework, thank God. I'd read every significant paper on stem cells in the last decade. Hundreds of articles, studies, trials…. He got that. He was happy to let us tag along.

Now, I had the physiological basis for how the stem cells worked and what I believed to be the best lab to deliver the most effective cells.

It was time to get the ball moving back home in my practice, so I could offer them to the many people who could benefit.

And so, it went.

Like with anything new in medicine, it started out on the fringe. The establishment always says: "You're crazy. This can't be done." Then, when it's proven that it can be done, the snake oil salesmen enter. So, even though it could be done, everyone was afraid to take the leap of faith. *Is this guy for real? Am I going to be screwed out of thousands with no one to turn to for recourse?* Then, one day, the doctors and scientists who had dedicated their lives to medical advancement were proven right. And they (we) are no longer perceived as crazy; we're heroes. Sometimes. Or for a short stint. We're heroes until something goes wrong….

Shortly after our visit to Stemell, I attended a regenerative medicine conference in Orlando. This was the first meeting I'd gone to in thirty years that was not devoted to surgery, either general or plastic. Up until then, my education was very conservative: college, medical school, general surgery residency, and then plastic surgery residency. I learned surgical principles and facts that were supported by multiple clinical studies by many different surgeons over many years, all bread and butter surgery. There was no experimental stuff, no preventative care; it was all therapy after the fact.

It didn't take long to realize that the attendees at the Orlando stem cell conference were not "our" people. This isn't a condescending comment. It was wild and cool because these people were taking giant risks, risks we've never taken with my practice.

In that conference, Chris and I felt the energy in the room. It was contagious. And we knew this would work. We'd known all along.

We'd contracted the "fever" from Peyman, from the regenerative medicine conference, from all the medical practitioners who were there, risking everything to help people. We needed to mix things up and get involved, because we've always been in the business of helping people. We've been searching for the answer to Marston's brain injury for years. We've read everything; we've traveled everywhere, talked to everyone, and tried every therapy we could find.

We knew we were capable of doing more than just helping our son. We knew we had to become one of those people from the conference—one of the trailblazers—if we were to see this through.

I could use stem cells for wound healing. That was my first thought. That was a no-brainer; I had already done the experimental procedure with great success.

This would be my angle to get into this community of trailblazers. Doctors all over the country were starting to use the umbilical cord, cutting it up and sewing it into wounds. I would start with what I knew. Then, I'd move into stem cell therapy for people with disorders and diseases for which they had been doing research, for which there was no cure or life-affecting treatment.

Chris and I saw this as our future without having so much as one real conversation about it prior to going to this conference.

19

STARTING OUR OWN CLINIC

WE ATTENDED OUR SECOND STEM cell conference in August in Miami. We could drive there, which was nice, and the doctor keynoting had been doing research with stem cells and eye disorders and diseases. I hadn't studied much on the subject, and so I figured it couldn't hurt. This proved to be an amazing watershed moment for us. This conference was more academic than experimental, but doctors who were educated and trained like me—and who had also jumped on the stem cell train—were in plentitude. The data was thought provoking and well presented. We met Peyman and his team. They were there to discuss and demonstrate why his stem cell products were superior to others.

One of the researchers presenting was Dr. Scheffer Tseng, an ophthalmologist/cellular biologist PhD and a groundbreaking researcher. He discussed how he restored sight to the blind through his work with stem cells. To say it was miraculous was an understatement. While Dr. Tseng presented, I turned to Chris and said, "I think I know him, or we're related somewhere on the educational family tree."

After the talk, I tracked him down, introduced myself, and congratulated him on a lifetime of work and on his ability to help those with chemical burns to the eyes. I told him I thought we were connected somehow, and we grabbed a cup of coffee.

"Have you ever been to the University of California, San Francisco?" he asked.

"I did my general surgery residency there."

He told me he was a PhD in Michael Harrison's lab. I told him I was Michael Harrison's resident on the Pediatric Surgery Service at Moffit Hospital. We must have met sometime. We certainly knew the same people.

He then said he left to attend John Hopkins Medical School, and then the University of Miami for ophthalmology residency. He became a surgical professor at Bascom Palmer Eye Institute. All he ever wanted to do was learn how to fix eyes. Bascom Palmer is one of the leading eye institutes in the world, and it was right here in Miami. Dr. Tseng was there in the early nineties, which was where I went from '92–'94. I left San Francisco to attend the University of Miami and had worked closely with the ophthalmologist at BPEI. We must have crossed paths again. The history of our medical family trees was very similar.

This led to a discussion of using stem cells in plastic surgery. He told me there was a plastic surgeon in Jacksonville, Florida who got incredible results on a patient with large, open groin wounds. I told him that was me. We laughed.

As it turned out, he founded the lab and company that makes Bio-Tissue® and Amniox. I had been using the end product of all his research.

I now knew the man behind the curtain.

This conference convinced me that stem cell therapy was going to be the next groundbreaking medical breakthrough. It will become the standard of care for a variety of illnesses, arthritis and metabolic syndrome, diabetes, aging, cerebral palsy, autism, Alzheimer's, and Parkinson's disease.

More Facts about Stem Cells:

As I mentioned in Chapter 14, there are various types of stem cells in umbilical cord blood. Some are mesenchymal, some are epithelial, some are endothelial, and some are hematopoietic. So, you're getting all of these when you use cord blood for stem cell replacement therapy. The process of extraction, centrifugation, and washing the cord blood has not yet been standardized, making every collection tedious and tricky. The extraction time and transport affect each batch, as does temperature.

When administering stem cells, the timing, dosing, and quality are more art than science. The dosage is determined by the weight of the patient, clinical response, and data from limited clinical studies, as well as animal studies.

Furthermore, these are live cells, making the procedure a true transplant. These cells are transported at -80° Centigrade (-112° Fahrenheit). They are cooled to slow metabolism and decrease the need for oxygen. Once thawed, the oxygen demand increases, and there's but a seven-minute window before they begin to die off. You have to really know what you're doing to administer these cells to a patient.

In Panama, Dr. Riordan uses his own lab to both process and administer stem cells. He takes the mesenchymal stem cells and expands them (causes them to divide) in a flask. He makes millions. This way, he can give more cells to more people. However, MSCs have a limited number of divisions before they lose effectiveness. It is unclear to me if this forced expansion of the MSC line is any better than the natural expansion seen in the body. In the US, though, it's against the law to expand cells. All the stem cells we currently use here are original, termed MMT (minimally manipulated tissue) by FDA decree.

Dr. Riordan believes these expanded MSCs are the golden ticket. He wants to give his patients more than what's just in the cord blood. He wants to give patients an injection that is 100 percent capable of decreasing inflammation, modulating the immune system, stimulating regeneration, and reducing scarring. This way, the potential benefit is tremendous. But the question is:

do you just give that type of stem cells, or do you give umbilical cord blood, which not only contains MSCs but a variety of other stem cells and immune-regulating cells? I do not believe there has been the necessary research to demonstrate one way is superior to the other.

(Check out the Autism Stem Cells 2.0 Facebook group and Autism Stem Cells 3.0 Facebook group to read up on this debate among the moms of autistic kids.)

I believe Dr. Neil Riordan is helping a lot of people, but his reports seem mostly anecdotal or derived from case studies; I haven't really seen any rigorous studies. Do not get me wrong; this is not a criticism. But, for me, these methods do not render enough hard evidence to guide dosage, cell line, cellular components, and timing of subsequent doses.

The Duke study was a phase I study. A phase I study is designed to make sure the therapy being tested is not harmful. The researchers used autologous (self) umbilical cord blood that had been stored from birth. There were no harmful side effects. In fact, the majority of subjects improved dramatically. Autism spectrum disorder is difficult to study, as the causes are unknown and there's no objective testing that can be measured and followed. Having said this, the researchers at Duke chose several well-known autism rating scales to use as markers. These included the Clinical Autism Rating Scale (CARS), Vineland Adaptive Behavior Scale, Aberrant Behavior Checklist (ABC), and others. They showed approximately

60 percent of children improved significantly and maintained their gains. Duke is currently recruiting for a phase II study on umbilical cord blood and autism. Phase II studies are studies that try to determine if the therapy actually works. Next comes a phase III study, which is designed to answer the question: Is this new therapy better than what we currently have? Finally, a phase IV study answers the question: What else do we need to know? Duke was the first top-of-the-line US medical center to study stem cells and their effect on autism. More medical centers will follow. It will take years to sort out all of the questions. But years and years is long way away if you have autism or you're a parent or caregiver of a person with autism.

We do know now that giving umbilical cord blood and stem cells is safe and has significant potential benefit.

Most insurance companies will not pay for anything experimental, and stem cell therapy is costly and considered experimental. It's done on a case-by-case basis as of this writing.

With my patient, Gail, she had been debilitated and needing daily nurse care for years. This is costly for Medicare. I convinced the hospital that treating her wounds with an umbilical cord implantation could result in her living on her own again, on being a productive and contributing member of society, saving Medicare hundreds of thousands of dollars in the long run. The hospital listened to my request and had the approval from Medicare in a timely fashion. They agreed to the procedure under a new Medicare law, the pass-through payment provision, which reimburses a hospital and staff for costs incurred during what's considered an "experimental" medical procedure. Congress developed this pass-through provision in 2015 to ensure forward motion with new drugs and medical procedures in medicine. (It costs about $100 million to test a new drug to get it ready for market; then, it hits stumbling blocks with insurance companies and with financing/marketing, so Congress stepped in.)

As you've read, the cost of acquiring stem cells is high, $500 to transport a single transfusion. We're not dealing with a pill, cream, or gel. Stem cells are living tissue and must be kept at -80° Celsius. They come individually packaged. For all these reasons, sustaining their viability is costly and not guaranteed, which is why industry standard for stem cell viability after transport is so low (40–60 percent).

It cost about $20,000 for Marston's first transfusion of stem cells in Chicago. Up to five follow-up procedures have been called for, depending on how he responds after each one.

Stemell vetted me as a provider, and Chris and I joined the trailblazers. There's a cost of doing business and a cost of expertise...and, if we were going to make our son part of the grand stem cell experiment, we were going to take the risk, too.

For one year, we studied everything on the logistics of administering stem cells. We traveled to labs, we trained ourselves, and we trained our employees. "God, we hope this is the right thing. We could have stayed a plastic surgery practice." Chris reiterated that more than once along our journey.

We officially added stem cell replacement to my practice in December 2018, administering the therapy treatments on Wednesdays. This means I no longer operate on Wednesdays. I'm in my late fifties (this side of retirement, if all goes well). More than a few people think we're nuts for doing this. After more thorough research, we've gone with Stemell. So far, their 92–95 percent viability success rate with stem cell transportation still can't be beat.

When these cells arrive in my office about ten a.m. on a Wednesday, I'm administering them intravenously by eleven or so. Everybody in the office—my team and the stem cell replacement therapy patients—is ready to go on the day of delivery. Literally nothing can go wrong…or thousands of dollars are flushed down the toilet.

I just administered Marston's fourth treatment right here in our office.

•º•º•

How long does it take to notice the effects of stem cell replacement therapy? Tough question. It's being tried on so many things right now, from cancer to autism to healing skin that's been ravaged by flesh-eating bacteria. From multiple studies, I believe most people will see results in two to three months. Anecdotally, parents may see things right away.

While riding his bike, my anesthesiologist got hit by a car a couple years ago. His physical injuries were so severe he had to retire from anesthesia. He walked with a limp and developed arthritis and other chronic pain in his back and hips.

He's a great candidate for this....

He signed up and got an infusion of cells. He reported feeling pretty good at two weeks. At a month, he felt so much better that he was trying to discount it to rule out the placebo effect. However, by two months, he was off all pain meds and had walked 15,000 pain-free steps—something he hadn't done in two years. We know stem cells target inflammation like heat-seeking missiles. They attacked his physical injuries on the cellular level and eradicated his inflammation. They also stimulated regeneration and decreased scarring. He sleeps better and has more energy.

We know the brains of autistic children are inflamed; their guts are inflamed, too. This shows up on brain scans and MRIs.

There is no way to grade Marston's progress or look at what is going on in his brain specifically. But as a parent, I have seen a significant and beautiful change. He is more organized. He speaks more clearly and is conversant. His time management has improved, as well as his ability to maintain a schedule. With all this happening, he has gained confidence and become more independent.

As a side note, I have not had one parent tell me they did not see an effect from the stem cells. In fact, most conversations are centered on when their child can have the next dose. I gave an eight-year-old boy his second infusion in April 2019. His first infusion had been about three months prior. It was a struggle. It took several people to hold him down. He was scared. He pulled his IV out, and we had to put it in again. Traumatic for all involved.

For his second infusion, he came in and hopped on the table without being told. He did not need to be held down. He was talkative and excited about getting a McDonald's Happy Meal after the procedure. He winced and cried for a couple of seconds when he was stuck, but he did not move. He was watching a movie during the infusion and was not fazed when the IV came out.

A completely different kid.

Stem cells work.

20

TWENTY-FOUR YEARS LATER

"I know the plans I have for you, plans to prosper you, and not to harm you, plans to give you hope and a future."

—Jeremiah 29:11

EVEN BEFORE I KNEW I WAS a warrior mom, I bought a baby pillow with that Bible quote on it when Marston was six months old, having no idea he would have special needs. This verse reminds me daily to remain optimistic and to have peace and hope for his future.

.°.°.°.

Imagine you got a puzzle for Christmas, but there's no picture on the front of the box. Then, imagine when you open the box and dump out all of the pieces, none of them look like regular puzzle pieces. On top of that, the box seems bottomless; the pieces just keeping coming like they're self-generating. You look at the outside of the box again and discover a disclaimer in very fine print: *This puzzle contains about five million pieces and takes, on average, twenty-five years to solve—working eight hours a day, seven days a week. No directions included. Do not start this puzzle unless you have the time and desire to finish it.* And then, in even smaller print, there is a warning: *Begin at your own risk, for you may go mad or die trying.*

We gave Marston his fourth dose of stem cells in December of 2018. You commit to three doses. If you don't see the results you were hoping for, the treatments are discontinued. However, if benefits are noticed, you can continue the therapy for up to six transfusions (as mentioned, dosing is based on cells and weight: one million cells per kilogram is the guide).

Marston continues to progress with each dose. It's powerful to watch him become more confident. He's venturing out into new activities, his diet has become more varied, he's begun to exercise on his own, and he's begun conversing at a more intimate level with friends and family.

We started this puzzle by connecting A to B, C to D, X to Y, and on and on we went. Since March 17, 1995, this has been our lives.

I believe we put our five-millionth piece in this year: stem cell therapy.

Having a child with special needs is a constant battle, emotionally, mentally, and physically. You are always battling to find the newest therapy or medical breakthrough that may be beneficial to your child. You're mentally battling your family and friends on your child's abilities, having to justify their limitations as well as your decisions on parenting. You battle the education system for services, individualized plans, and therapies. Your heart aches for your child daily because of their isolation and endless limitations. My biggest battle has always been within my own mind: Did I fight the good fight? Did I do all I could? Did I leave anything on the table?

To my fellow warrior moms, I honor all of you in this battle. We are in an army we did not volunteer for; it was a draft. I stand side by side with you in this war, never surrendering.

Today, as I write this last line—on March 17, 2019, Marston's twenty-fourth birthday—his future is becoming brighter and brighter.

Don't ever give up hope.

RECOMMENDED ARTICLES ON AUTISM AND STEM CELLS

"Neuroglial Activation and Neuroinflammation in the Brain of Patients with Autism"

Diana L. Vargas, MD, Caterina Nascimbene, MD, Chitra Krishnan, MHS, Andrew W. Zimmerman, MD, and Carlos A. Pardo, MD

Autism is a neurodevelopmental disorder characterized by impaired communication and social interaction and may be accompanied by mental retardation and epilepsy. Its cause remains unknown, despite evidence that genetic, environmental, and immunological factors may play a role in its pathogenesis. To investigate whether immune-mediated mechanisms are involved in the pathogenesis of autism, we used immunocytochemistry, cytokine protein arrays, and enzyme-linked immunosorbent assays to study brain tissues and cerebrospinal fluid (CSF) from autistic patients and determined the magnitude of neuroglial and inflammatory reactions and their cytokine expression profiles. Brain tissues from cerebellum, midfrontal, and cingulate gyrus obtained at autopsy from 11 patients with autism were used for morphological studies. Fresh-frozen tissues available from seven patients and CSF from six living autistic patients were used for cytokine protein profiling. We demonstrate an active neuroinflammatory process in the cerebral cortex, white matter, and notably in cerebellum of autistic patients. Immunocytochemical studies showed marked activation of microglia and astroglia, and cytokine profiling indicated that macrophage chemoattractant protein (MCP)–1 and tumor growth factor–β1, derived from neuroglia, were the most prevalent cytokines in brain tissues. CSF showed a unique proinflammatory profile of cytokines, including a marked increase in MCP-1. Our findings indicate that innate neuroimmune reactions play a pathogenic role in an undefined proportion of autistic patients, suggesting that future therapies might involve modifying neuroglial responses in the brain.

For access to the full version of this article, go to:
https://onlinelibrary.wiley.com/doi/pdf/10.1002/ana.20315

"The Role of Immune Dysfunction in the Pathophysiology of Autism"

Onore C., Careaga M., Ashwood P.

Autism spectrum disorders (ASD) are a complex group of neurodevelopmental disorders encompassing impairments in communication, social interactions and restricted stereotypical behaviors. Although a link between altered immune responses and ASD was first recognized nearly 40 years ago, only recently has new evidence started to shed light on the complex multifaceted relationship between immune dysfunction and behavior in ASD. Neurobiological research in ASD has highlighted pathways involved in neural development, synapse plasticity, structural brain abnormalities, cognition and behavior. At the same time, several lines of evidence point to altered immune dysfunction in ASD that directly impacts some or all these neurological processes. Extensive alterations in immune function have now been described in both children and adults with ASD, including ongoing inflammation in brain specimens, elevated pro-inflammatory cytokine profiles in the CSF and blood, increased presence of brain-specific auto-antibodies and altered immune cell function. Furthermore, these dysfunctional immune responses are associated with increased impairments in behaviors characteristic of core features of ASD, in particular, deficits in social interactions and communication. This accumulating evidence suggests that immune processes play a key role in the pathophysiology of ASD. This review will discuss the current state of our knowledge of immune dysfunction in ASD, how these findings may impact on underlying neuro-immune mechanisms and implicate potential areas where the manipulation of the immune response could have an impact on behavior and immunity in ASD.

This link will take you to the full version of this article:
https://www.ncbi.nlm.nih.gov/pmc/articles/PMC3418145/

The publisher's final edited PDF version of this article is available for purchase at:
https://www.sciencedirect.com/science/article/pii/S0889159111004922?via%3Dihub

"Autologous Cord Blood Infusions Are Safe and Feasible in Young Children with Autism Spectrum Disorder: Results of a Single-Center Phase I Open-Label Trial"

Geraldine Dawson, Jessica M. Sun, Katherine S. Davlantis, Michael Murias, Lauren Franz, Jesse Troy, Ryan Simmons, Maura Sabatos-Devito, Rebecca Durham, Joanne Kurtzberg

—SIGNIFICANCE STATEMENT—

This phase I study demonstrates that it is safe and feasible to perform autologous umbilical cord blood infusions in young children with autism spectrum disorder and identifies several promising outcome measures for use in future trials.

Despite advances in early diagnosis and behavioral therapies, more effective treatments for children with autism spectrum disorder (ASD) are needed. We hypothesized that umbilical cord blood-derived cell therapies may have potential in alleviating ASD symptoms by modulating inflammatory processes in the brain. Accordingly, we conducted a phase I, open-label trial to assess the safety and feasibility of a single intravenous infusion of autologous umbilical cord blood, as well as sensitivity to change in several ASD assessment tools, to determine suitable endpoints for future trials. Twenty-five children, median age 4.6 years (range 2.26–5.97), with a confirmed diagnosis of ASD and a qualified banked autologous umbilical cord blood unit, were enrolled. Children were evaluated with a battery of behavioral and functional tests immediately prior to cord blood infusion (baseline) and 6 and 12 months later. Assessment of adverse events across the 12-

month period indicated that the treatment was safe and well tolerated. Significant improvements in children's behavior were observed on parent-report measures of social communication skills and autism symptoms, clinician ratings of overall autism symptom severity and degree of improvement, standardized measures of expressive vocabulary, and objective eye-tracking measures of children's attention to social stimuli, indicating that these measures may be useful endpoints in future studies. Behavioral improvements were observed during the first 6 months after infusion and were greater in children with higher baseline nonverbal intelligence quotients. These data will serve as the basis for future studies to determine the efficacy of umbilical cord blood infusions in children with ASD.

To read the article in its entirety, go to Stem Cells Journals: https://stemcellsjournals.onlinelibrary.wiley.com/doi/full/10.1002/sctm.16-0474

"Transplantation of Human Cord Blood Mononuclear Cells and Umbilical Cord-derived Mesenchymal Stem Cells in Autism"

Yong-Tao Lv, Yun Zhang, Min Liu, Jia-na-ti Qiuwaxi, Paul Ashwood, Sungho Charles Cho, Ying Huan, Ru-Cun Ge, Xing-Wang Chen, Zhao-Jing Wang, Byung-Jo Kim, and Xiang Hu

Autism is a pervasive neurodevelopmental disorder. At present there are no defined mechanisms of pathogenesis and therapy is mostly limited to behavioral interventions. Stem cell transplantation may offer a unique treatment strategy for autism due to immune and neural dysregulation observed in this disease. This non-randomized, open-label, single center phase I/II trial investigated the safety and efficacy of combined transplantation of human cord blood mononuclear cells (CBMNCs) and umbilical cord-derived mesenchymal stem cells (UCMSCs) in treating children with autism. 37 subjects diagnosed with autism were enrolled into this study and divided into three groups: CBMNC group (14 subjects, received CBMNC transplantation and rehabilitation therapy), Combination group (9 subjects, received both CBMNC and UCMSC transplantation and rehabilitation therapy), and Control group (14 subjects, received only rehabilitation therapy). Transplantations included four stem cell infusions through intravenous and intrathecal injections once a week. Treatment safety was evaluated with laboratory examinations and clinical assessment of adverse effects. The Childhood Autism Rating Scale (CARS), Clinical Global Impression (CGI) scale and Aberrant Behavior Checklist (ABC) were adopted to assess the therapeutic efficacy at baseline (pre-treatment) and following treatment. There were no significant safety issues related to the treatment and no observed severe adverse effects. Statistically significant differences were shown on CARS, ABC scores and CGI evaluation in the two treatment groups compared to the control at 24 weeks post-treatment (p < 0.05). Transplantation of CBMNCs demonstrated efficacy compared to the control group; however, the combination of CBMNCs and UCMSCs showed larger therapeutic effects than the CBMNC transplantation alone. There were no safety issues noted during infusion and the whole monitoring period. ClinicalTrials.gov: NCT01343511, Title "Safety and Efficacy of Stem Cell Therapy in Patients with Autism."

https://europepmc.org/abstract/med/23978163

The rest of this article is free online at: https://translational-medicine.biomedcentral.com/articles/10.1186/1479-5876-11-196

"The Potential of Cord Blood Stem Cells for Use in Regenerative Medicine"

David T Harris, Michael Badowski, Nafees Ahmad & Mohamed A. Gaballa

It is estimated that up to 128 million individuals might benefit from regenerative medicine therapy, or almost 1 in 3 individuals in the US. If accurate, the need to relieve suffering and reduce healthcare costs is an enormous motivator to rapidly bring stem cell therapies to the clinic. Unfortunately, embryonic stem (ES) cell therapies are limited at present by ethical and political constraints and, most importantly, by significant biologic hurdles. Thus, for the foreseeable future, the march of regenerative medicine to the clinic will depend on the development of non-ES cell therapies. At present, non-ES cells easily available in large numbers can be found in the bone marrow, adipose tissue and umbilical cord blood (CB). Each of these stem cells is being used to treat a variety of diseases. This review shows that CB contains multiple populations of pluripotent stem cells, and can be considered the best alternative to ES cells. CB stem cells are capable of giving rise to hematopoietic, epithelial, endothelial and neural tissues both in vitro and in vivo. Thus, CB stem cells are amenable to treat a wide variety of diseases including cardiovascular, ophthalmic, orthopedic, neurologic and endocrine diseases.

https://arizona.pure.elsevier.com/en/publications/the-potential-of-cord-blood-stem-cells-for-use-in-regenerative-me

The full article is available for purchase at:
https://www.tandfonline.com/doi/full/10.1517/14712598.7.9.1311?scroll=top&needAccess=true

REFERENCES & RESOURCES

Introduction

The first case of autism: Zucker, John Donvan and Caren. "The Early History of Autism in America." Smithsonian.com. January 1, 2016. Accessed April 5, 2019.
https://www.smithsonianmag.com/science-nature/early-history-autism-america-180957684/.

Autism used to affect 1/10,000 babies: "Facts and Statistics." Autism Society. Accessed April 10, 2019.
http://www.autism-society.org/what-is/facts-and-statistics/.

Chapter 1: Life in Fifth Gear

9 **I'm 100 percent for vaccinations:** "Can Immunizations Be Given Individually?" Focus for Health. February 7, 2019. Accessed July 11, 2019. https://www.focusforhealth.org/can-immunizations-be-given-individually/.

9 **Medical research journalist Neil Z. Miller:** Miller, Neil Z. "Combining Childhood Vaccines at One Visit Is Not Safe." *Journal of American Physicians and Surgeons.* Vol. 21. No. 2. 47–49. Summer 2016. Accessed July 10, 2019. https://www.jpands.org/vol21no2/miller.pdf.

10 **Multi-dose vaccines require preservatives:** Center for Biologics Evaluation and Research. "Thimerosal and Vaccines." U.S. Food and Drug Administration. Accessed July 11, 2019.
https://www.fda.gov/vaccines-blood-biologics/safety-availability-biologics/thimerosal-and-vaccines.

10 **Additionally, "Single-dose vaccine formats can:** Lee, Bruce Y., Bryan A. Norman, Tina-Marie Assi, Sheng-I Chen, Rachel R. Bailey, Jayant Rajgopal, Shawn T. Brown, Ann E. Wiringa, and Donald S. Burke. "Single versus Multi-Dose Vaccine Vials: An Economic Computational Model." *National Center for*

Biotechnology Information, U.S. National Library of Medicine. June 3, 2010. Accessed July 11, 2019.
https://www.ncbi.nlm.nih.gov/pmc/articles/PMC2919154/.

11 **The first hepatitis B vaccine became:** "What is the History of Hepatitis B Vaccine Use in America?" National Vaccine Information Center. Accessed July 11, 2019.
https://www.nvic.org/vaccines-and-diseases/hepatitis-b/vaccine-history.aspx.

12 **In 2002, it became mandatory:** "Perinatal Hepatitis B Prevention Program Resource Manual." Florida Department of Health. Accessed July 11, 2019.
http://www.floridahealth.gov/diseases-and-conditions/perinatal-hepatitis-b/_documents/phbpp-resource-guide.pdf.

12 **But, in a cross-sectional study:** Gallagher, Caroline M. and Melody S. Goodman. 2010. "Hepatitis B Vaccination of Male Neonates and Autism Diagnosis, NHIS 1997–2002." *Journal of Toxicology and Environmental Health*, Part A, 73:24, 1665-1677.
https://www.tandfonline.com/doi/abs/10.1080/15287394.2010.519317?src=recsys&journalCode=uteh20.

13 **In the early 1950s, four:** "Vaccine History: Developments by Year." Reviewed by Paul A. Offit, MD on March 07, 2019. Accessed July 11, 2019.
https://www.chop.edu/centers-programs/vaccine-education-center/vaccine-history/developments-by-year.

13 **Even now, with vaccinations in:** Guzman, Timothy Alexander. "Big Pharma and Big Profits: The Multibillion Dollar Vaccine Market." *Global Research.* January 27, 2016. Accessed July 11, 2019.
https://www.globalresearch.ca/big-pharma-and-big-profits-the-multibillion-dollar-vaccine-market/5503945.

14 **For anyone interested in learning:** Cave, Stephanie. 2010. *What Your Doctor May Not Tell You About™ Children's Vaccinations.* New York, New York: Grand Central Life & Style.

Chapter 2: No One Left Behind

20 **In 1918, Rose (Fitzgerald) Kennedy:** Gordon, Meryl. "'Rosemary: The Hidden Kennedy Daughter,' by Kate Clifford Larson." *New York Times.* June 14, 2018. Accessed April 5, 2019.
https://www.nytimes.com/2015/10/11/books/review/rosemary-the-hidden-kennedy-daughter-by-kate-clifford-larson.html.

21 **The cure for Rosemary:** Gordon, Meryl. "'Rosemary: The Hidden Kennedy Daughter,' by Kate Clifford Larson." *New York Times.* June 14, 2018. Accessed April 5, 2019.
https://www.nytimes.com/2015/10/11/books/review/rosemary-the-hidden-kennedy-daughter-by-kate-clifford-larson.html.

21 **Shortly after Rosemary's lobotomy:** "History of Autism Blame. | Refrigerator Mothers | POV | PBS." POV. January 18, 2002. Accessed April 15, 2019.
http://archive.pov.org/refrigeratormothers/fridge/.

Chapter 3: The Wonder Years

29 **At around six months old:** Gymboree Play & Music. Accessed April 5, 2019.
Website: https://www.gymboreeclasses.com/.
Phone: 415.604.3094

30 **When Marston turned one:** "Neurology at Highland Hospital." What Is a Neurologist? – Neurology – Highland Hospital – University of Rochester Medical Center. Accessed April 5, 2019.
https://www.urmc.rochester.edu/highland/departments-centers/neurology/what-is-a-neurologist.aspx.

30 **But, we decided to have genetic testing:** "What Is Genetic Testing?" Facts. November 13, 2014. Accessed April 5, 2019.
https://www.yourgenome.org/facts/what-is-genetic-testing.

30 **...as well as a hearing test:** "What Is a Hearing Test?" Hearing Link. Accessed April 5, 2019.
https://www.hearinglink.org/your-hearing/what-is-a-hearing-test/.

30 **By eighteen months, when I:** "Speech Therapy." Autism Speaks. Accessed April 5, 2019.
https://www.autismspeaks.org/speech-therapy.

31 **In January of 1997, when:** "Music Classes for Children and Schools." Kindermusik. Accessed April 5, 2019.
Website: https://www.kindermusik.com/.
Phone: 1.800.628.5687
Email: info@kindermusik.com

32 **Concurrently, we started Mommy & Me:** "Mommy and Me Classes." Kindermusik. Accessed April 16, 2019.
Website: https://www.kindermusik.com/pg/mommy_and_me_classes.
Phone: 1.800.628.5687
Email: info@kindermusik.com

32 **Just before Marston was two:** "Accotink's Approach." Accotink Academy. Accessed April 5, 2019.
Website: http://accotinktherapeuticday.com/accotinks-approach/.
Phone: 703.451.8041
Email: james.corley@accotink.com

37 **These are some symptoms that:** "Signs of Autism." National Autism Association. Accessed April 5, 2019.
http://nationalautismassociation.org/resources/signs-of-autism/.

Chapter 5: This Is Bad

51 **Several people tossed around the:** Logsdon, Ann. "Defining Attention Deficit Disorder (ADD) Without Hyperactivity." Verywell Mind. Accessed April 6, 2019.
https://www.verywellmind.com/add-and-attention-deficit-disorders-2161810.

Chapter 6: This Program Is No Joke

56 **The Institutes for the Achievement:** "IAHP." The Institutes for the Achievement of Human Potential. Accessed April 6, 2019.
Website: https://www.iahp.org/.
Phone: 215.233.2050
Email: institutes@iahp.org

57 **Glenn was a war hero:** "About Glenn Doman, Founder of The Institutes." The Institutes for the Achievement of Human Potential. Accessed April 6, 2019.
https://www.iahp.org/about-us/about-glenn-doman.

59 **Hundreds of thousands of parents:** "About The Institutes for the Achievement of Human Potential." The Institutes for the Achievement of Human Potential. Accessed April 6, 2019. https://www.iahp.org/about-us.

59 **The Institutes believes there is:** "Early Child Development." The Institutes for the Achievement of Human Potential. Accessed April 6, 2019. https://www.iahp.org/early-development/.

60 **The first thing that happens:** "About The Institutes for the Achievement of Human Potential." The Institutes for the Achievement of Human Potential. Accessed April 6, 2019.
https://www.iahp.org/about-us.

62 **Most people don't know the:** "Non-Drug Alternatives for Seizures." [Go to the Front Page.] Autism One. Accessed April 6, 2019.
http://www.autismone.org/content/non-drug-alternatives-seizures.

64 **We worked on patterning daily:** "What is patterning? A Technique Taught by Dr. Glen [Glenn] Doman." RSS. Accessed April 6, 2019.
http://www.huletsmith.com/post/what-is-patterning-a-technique-taught-by-dr-glen-doman1.

66 **Brachiation is the final exercise:** P., Danny and Kristi Johnson. "The Power of Brachiating." Maximum Training Solutions. January 10, 2018. Accessed April 6, 2019.
http://www.maximumtrainingsolutions.com/power-brachiating/.

70   **The first thing they tell:** "Why Dairy Products Are Harmful for Your Child." The Institutes for the Achievement of Human Potential. Accessed April 6, 2019.
http://www.iahp.org/dairy/.

70   **The Institutes understands we've been:** "Why Dairy Products Are Harmful for Your Child." The Institutes for the Achievement of Human Potential. Accessed April 6, 2019.
http://www.iahp.org/dairy/.

Chapter 7: Socialization Does Matter

80   **From age three to age:** "Social Development in 3-5 Year Olds." Scholastic. Accessed April 10, 2019.
https://www.scholastic.com/parents/family-life/social-emotional-learning/development-milestones/social-development-3-5-year-olds.html.

80   **Montessori schools specialize in independent:** "Montessori Resources for Schools, Teachers, Families and Parents." American Montessori Society. Website: https://amshq.org/.
Phone: 212.358.1250
Email: ams@amshq.org

81   **Everything that happens with our:** "Brain Anatomy, Anatomy of the Human Brain." Mayfieldclinic.com. Accessed April 10, 2019.
https://mayfieldclinic.com/pe-anatbrain.htm.

81   **By the time a child:** Rosen, Peg. "The Importance of Emotional Intelligence for Kids with Learning and Attention Issues." Accessed April 10, 2019.
https://www.understood.org/en/friends-feelings/empowering-your-child/building-on-strengths/the-importance-of-emotional-intelligence-for-kids-with-learning-and-attention-issues.

82   **I want to explain briefly:** Reichlin, Analiisa. "The Importance of Repetition in Child Development." Kindermusik. December 13, 2011. Accessed April 10, 2019.
https://www.kindermusik.com/mindsonmusic/parenting-tips/the-importance-of-repetition-in-child-development/.

82 **When a nerve signal reaches:** Cherry, Kendra. "The Role of Neurotransmitters." Verywell Mind. Updated March 12, 2019. Accessed April 8, 2019.
https://www.verywellmind.com/what-is-a-neurotransmitter-2795394.

83 **Because your baby is rapidly:** "Brain Development of Children from 0-6 Years – Facts Every Parent Should Know." ADAM & Mila. October 18, 2018. Accessed April 8, 2019.
https://www.adam-mila.com/brain-development-children-0-6-years/.

86 **The decision did not come:** "Montessori Education at Montessori Discovery School." Montessori Discovery School. Accessed April 8, 2019.
http://www.montdiscovery.org/.

Chapter 8: Stronger Together

90 **We started meeting to exchange:** "Heal Autism Now | Helping Enrich Autistic Lives | HEAL Foundation." Heal Autism Now | Helping Enrich Autistic Lives | HEAL Foundation. Accessed April 8, 2019.
http://www.healautismnow.org/.

91 **The Tomatis® Method uses unanticipated:** "Tomatis® Method, Auditory Stimulation Program for Improving Brain Functions." TOMATIS®. Accessed April 16, 2019.
https://www.tomatis.com/en.

92 **We discovered a Dr. Stanley:** Greenspan, Stanley and Diane Lewis. 2005. *The Affect-Based Language Curriculum (ABLC).* Interdisciplinary Council on Developmental and Learning Disorders.

92 **The Hill Academic Center:**
Website: https://www.hillcenter.org/.
Phone: 919.489.7464
Email: info@hillcenter.org

93 **Another intervention program we signed:**
Website: http://valeriedejean.org/

93 **In 2006, we discovered Play:** "How We Help." Play Attention. Accessed April 16, 2019.
Website: http://www.playattention.com/.
Phone: 1.800.788.6786

93 **In 2008, we reenrolled Marston:** "Sensory Learning." Sensory Learning. Accessed April 16, 2019.
Website: https://www.sensorylearning.com/.
Phone: 303.652.0588

93 **Dr. Harry Wachs was another renowned:** "Dr. Harry Wachs Obituary – Silver Spring, MD." Dignity Memorial. Accessed April 16, 2019.
https://www.dignitymemorial.com/obituaries/silver-spring-md/harry-wachs-7025377.

94 **This experience was delineated in:** Furth, Hans G. and Harry Wachs. 1975. *Thinking Goes to School: Piaget's Theory in Practice.* New York: Oxford University Press.

95 **He co-authored his second and:** Weider, Serena and Harry Wachs. 2012. *Visual/Spatial Portals to Thinking, Feeling and Movement: Advancing Competencies and Emotional Development in Children with Learning and Autism Spectrum Disorders.* Mendham, New Jersey: Profectum Foundation.

Chapter 10: The Power of Words

106 **In 1997, the reauthorization of:** Dybvik, Ann Christy. "Autism and the Inclusion Mandate." Education Next. January 11, 2017. Accessed April 10, 2019.
https://www.educationnext.org/autismandtheinclusionmandate/.

107 **Having a hired aide, a:** Giangreco, Michael F., Carter S. Smith, and Eliane Pinckney. "Addressing the Paraprofessional Dilemma in an Inclusive School: A Program Description." *Research & Practice for Persons with Severe Disabilities.* (2006) Vol. 31. No. 3, 215–229.
https://www.uvm.edu/sites/default/files/Center-on-Disability-and-Community-Inclusion/Giangrecorps31303.pdf.

108 **Even after stats on autism:** "Data and Statistics on Autism Spectrum Disorder." Centers for Disease Control and Prevention. Accessed April 10, 2019.
https://www.cdc.gov/ncbddd/autism/data.html.

109 **So, from 2003–2004, Marston:** "Center Academy." Center Academy. Accessed April 10, 2019.
http://centeracademy.com/.
Website: http://centeracademy.com.
Phone: 727.541.5716

111 **Our efforts in developing this:** "Dr. Marion Blank." Reading Kingdom. Accessed April 10, 2019.
https://www.readingkingdom.com/company/drblank.

111 **Dr. Blank had made a:** "Dr. Marion Blank." Reading Kingdom. Accessed April 10, 2019.
https://www.readingkingdom.com/company/drblank.

111 **Other works like *The Reading*:** Blank, Marion. 2006. *The Reading Remedy: Six Essential Skills That Will Turn Your Child into a Reader.* San Francisco, California: Jossey-Bass.

111 ***Spectacular Bond:*** Blank, Marion, Suzanne Goh, and Susan Deland. 2013. *Spectacular Bond: Reaching the Child with Autism.* San Diego, California: MSB Press.

111 ***ASD Typing:*** Blank, Marion and Suzanne Goh. 2014. *ASD Typing: A Program to Build Language Through Typing.* CreateSpace Independent Publishing Platform.

112 **She is the recipient of:** "Dr. Marion Blank." HuffPost. Accessed April 10, 2019.
https://www.huffpost.com/author/dr-marion-blank.

112 **Upton Sinclair Award:** "Dr. Marion Blank." HuffPost. Accessed April 10, 2019.
https://www.huffpost.com/author/dr-marion-blank.

112 **Special Education Software Award:** "Dr. Marion Blank." HuffPost. Accessed April 10, 2019.
https://www.huffpost.com/author/dr-marion-blank.

115 **She has always argued that:** "Learn About the Six Skill Integrated Method." Reading Kingdom. Accessed April 10, 2019.
https://www.readingkingdom.com/pages/six-skill-integrated-method.

116 **Dr. Marion Blank's method uses:** "Learn About the Six Skill Integrated Method." Reading Kingdom. Accessed April 10, 2019.
https://www.readingkingdom.com/pages/six-skill-integrated-method.

116 **Reading is commonly dissected into:** "Our Approach to Reading." ASD Reading. Accessed April 10, 2019.
https://www.asdreading.com/teachers/approach.

116 ***Ido in Autismland:*** Kedar, Ido. 2012. *Ido in Autismland: Climbing Out of Autism's Silent Prison.* Published by Sharon Kedar.

116 ***Carly's Voice: Breaking through Autism:*** Fleischmann, Arthur and Carly Fleischmann. 2012. *Carly's Voice: Breaking through Autism.* New York, New York: Touchstone.

117 **Facilitative communication, developed at Syracuse:** "The Institute on Communication and Inclusion." Syracuse University Institute on Communication and Inclusion. Accessed April 10, 2019.
http://ici.syr.edu/.

Chapter 12: What comes after "hi"?

128 **The term *executive functions* refers:** "Executive Functions." Executive Functions – an Overview | ScienceDirect Topics. Accessed April 10, 2019. https://www.sciencedirect.com/topics/neuroscience/executive-functions.

133 **We signed him up for horseback:** "Hypotherapy." Mountains of Costa Daurada. Accessed April 16, 2019. http://www.muntanyescostadaurada.cat/en/hipoterapia.

131 **Dog companion therapy is really:** "Service Dogs for Children." NEADS World Class Service Dogs. Accessed April 16, 2019. https://neads.org/service-dog-programs/service-dogs-for-children/?utm_source=google&utm_medium=cpc&gclid=CjwKCAjw-ZvlBRBbEiwANw9UWv0YHLbWZJ3cxDsf5HXU7b9poaHWA807q_JAr3vsw1cByp04QpcWnBoCLWQQAvD_BwE.

134 **Taekwondo: He studied this martial:** Kim, Yumi, Teri Todd, Takuto Fujii, Jae-Chun Lim, Konstantinos Vrongistinos, and Taeyou Jung. "Effects of Taekwondo Intervention on Balance in Children with Autism Spectrum Disorder." *Journal of Exercise Rehabilitation.* Vol. 12(4): 314–319. August 31, 2016. Accessed April 16, 2019. https://www.ncbi.nlm.nih.gov/pmc/articles/PMC5031378/.

134 **My favorite extracurricular activity:** "Ballroom Dance: Powerful Steps Beyond Autism." Fred Astaire Dance Studio Blog. July 11, 2012. Accessed April 16, 2019. http://fred-astaire.blogspot.com/2012/07/ballroom-dance-powerful-steps-beyond.html.

Chapter 13: I Wish the Whole World Was Like This

139 **Maplebrook Postsecondary School in Amenia:** Website: https://www.maplebrookschool.org/academics/post-secondary-program/. Phone: 845.373.9511 Email: admissions@maplebrookeschool.org

143 **The Arc Jacksonville (Arc) is a nonprofit:**
Website: https://www.arcjacksonville.org/.
Phone: 904.355.0155
Email: info@arcjacksonville.org

145 **As of this writing, Marston attends:**
Website: https://www.unf.edu/oncampustransition/.
Phone: 904.620.3890
Email: coeoct@unf.edu

145 **In 2007, ARC partnered with:** "The Arc Jacksonville On Campus Transition at UNF." UNF. Accessed April 16, 2019.
https://www.unf.edu/oncampustransition/.

Chapter 14: The Science behind Stem Cells

151 **On Chris's prompting, I watched:** Riordan, Neil H. 2017. *Stem Cell Therapy: A Rising Tide: How Stem Cells Are Disrupting Medicine and Transforming Lives.*

151 **Dr. Neil Riordan is an American:** "Neil Riordan, PA, PhD." Riordan Medical Institute. October 3, 2018. Accessed April 16, 2019.
https://rmiclinic.com/about/dr-neil-riordan/.

151 **This can be a very detailed:** Mayo Clinic Staff. "Frequently Asked Questions about Stem Cell Research." Mayo Clinic. April 2, 2019. Accessed April 16, 2019.
https://www.mayoclinic.org/tests-procedures/bone-marrow-transplant/in-depth/stem-cells/art-20048117.

152 **This simple experiment was pivotal:** American Federation of Aging Research. "Could a Little Young Blood Reverse the Effects of Aging?" MarketWatch. May 30, 2018. Accessed April 16, 2019.
https://www.marketwatch.com/story/could-a-little-young-blood-reverse-the-affects-of-aging-2018-05-30.

156 **Another source, and potentially the:** "What Are Umbilical Cord Stem Cells?" Stem Cells Australia. Accessed April 16, 2019.
http://www.stemcellsaustralia.edu.au/About-Stem-Cells/FAQ/What-are-umbilical-cord-stem-cells-.aspx.

159 **More evidence of inflammation being:** "Microglial Function in the Healthy Brain." The Green Lab. Accessed April 16, 2019. https://faculty.sites.uci.edu/kimgreen/bio/microglia-in-the-healthy-brain/.

161 **This data all points to a:** Masi, Anne, Nicholas Glozier, Russell Dale, and Adam J. Guastella. "The Immune System, Cytokines, and Biomarkers in Autism Spectrum Disorder." *Neuroscience Bulletin.* Vol. 33(2): 194–204. February 27, 2015. Accessed April 16, 2019. https://www.ncbi.nlm.nih.gov/pmc/articles/PMC5360854/.

162 **Stem cell therapy studies are:** "National MS Society Research in Stem Cells." National Multiple Sclerosis Society. March 11, 2019. Accessed April 16, 2019. https://www.nationalmssociety.org/Research/Research-News-Progress/Stem-Cells-in-MS/National-MS-Society-Research-in-Stem-Cells.

162 **But, because our stem cell supply:** Ahmed, Abu Shufian Ishtiaq, Matilda Hc Sheng, Samiksha Wasnik, David J. Baylink, and Kin-Hing William Lau. "Effect of Aging on Stem Cells." *World Journal of Experimental Medicine.* Vol. 7(1): 1–10. February 20, 2017. Accessed April 16, 2019. https://www.ncbi.nlm.nih.gov/pmc/articles/PMC5316899/.

162 **As it turns out, the:** Kern, Susanne, Hermann Eichler, Johannes Stoeve, Harald Klüter, and Karen Bieback. "Comparative Analysis of Mesenchymal Stem Cells from Bone Marrow, Umbilical Cord Blood, or Adipose Tissue." STEM CELLS. January 12, 2009. Accessed April 16, 2019. https://stemcellsjournals.onlinelibrary.wiley.com/doi/full/10.1634/stemcells.2005-0342.

163 **In other countries, such as:** Curran, Kevin. "Keeping up with Stem Cell Therapies." Rising Tide Biology. January 12, 2019. Accessed April 16, 2019. https://www.risingtidebio.com/history-stem-cell-therapy-benefits/.

164 **The first use was in the treatment:** "Top 50 Most Influential People on Stem Cells Today." World Stem Cells and Regenerative Medicine Congress. https://www.cirm.ca.gov/sites/default/files/files/press_release/Top_50_Global_Stem_Cell_Influencers.pdf.

Chapter 15: Stem Cell Replacement Therapy Options for Marston

167   **I went to Dr. Lobe's website:** "Regenerative Medicine – Anti Aging Treatments Chicago." Regenevéda. Accessed April 16, 2019. https://regeneveda.com/.

Chapter 17: More Evidence on the Potential of Stem Cells

178   **The product is called Amniox:** "Our Story." Our Story | Restorative Tissue Products | AmnioxMedical.com. Accessed May 21, 2019. https://amnioxmedical.com/our-story/.

180   **These are generic cells, and the:** "Multimedia Encyclopedia – Penn State Hershey Medical Center – Stem Cell Research." Penn State Hershey Health Information Library. Accessed May 21, 2019. http://pennstatehershey.adam.com/content.aspx?productId=117&pid=1&gid=007120.

181   **That's when he told me about:** "Allogenic Umbilical Cord Stem Cells and Exosome Products." Stemell. Accessed May 21, 2019. https://stemell.com/.

Chapter 18: Stemell

184   **There is significant experimental and:** Wang, Sen, Hongbin Cheng, Guanghui Dai, Xiaodong Wang, Rongrong Hua, Xuebin Liu, Peishen Wang, Guangming Chen, Wu Yue, Yiahua An. "Umbilical Cord Mesenchymal Stem Cell Transplantation Significantly Improves Neurological Function in Patients with Sequelae of Traumatic Brain Injury." *ScienceDirect*. 76–84. August 11, 2013. Accessed April 16, 2019. http://northfloridastemcells.com/wp-content/uploads/TBI.pdf.

184   **There were a handful to choose:** "About – Stem Cells and Stem Therapy." Stemell. Accessed April 16, 2019. https://stemell.com/about/.

Chapter 19: Starting Our Own Clinic

192 **Bascom Palmer is one of:**
Website: https://umiamihealth.org/bascom-palmer-eye-institute.
Phone: 305.243.4357
Email: heretohelp@med.miami.edu

193 **As it turned out, he founded:** "About Us – Promoting Natural Healing through Science." Biotissue. Accessed April 16, 2019.
https://www.biotissue.com/about/about-biotissue.aspx.
Website: https://www.biotissue.com/default.aspx.
Phone: 1.888.296.8858
Email: info@biotissue.com

194 **Dr. Riordan believes these expanded MSCs:** Gudleviciene, Zivile, Gabrielis Kundrotas, Regina Liudkeviciene, Jelena Rascon, and Marcin Jurga. "Quick and Effective Method of Bone Marrow Mesenchymal Stem Cell Extraction." *Open Medicine* (Warsaw, Poland). Vol. 10(1): 44–49. October 8, 2014. Accessed April 16, 2019.
https://www.ncbi.nlm.nih.gov/pmc/articles/PMC5152963/.

194 **In Panama, Dr. Riordan uses:** "Riordan-McKenna Institute Archives." Stem Cell Institute. Accessed May 21, 2019.
https://www.cellmedicine.com/stem-cell-therapy/news/riordan-mckenna-institute/.

195 **They showed approximately 60 percent:** Khanna, Samiha and Duke Health News. "Experimental Cord Blood Therapy for Autism Studied." Duke Department of Pediatrics. Accessed June 12, 2019.
https://pediatrics.duke.edu/news/experimental-cord-blood-therapy-autism-studied.

197 **Stemell vetted me as a provider:**
Website: http://northfloridastemcells.com.
Phone: 904.215.5800
Email: NFLstemcells@gmail.com

INDEX